Praise for *A Love Affair with the Unknown*

"A vulnerable, creative, and lyrical memoir about the human condition."

—*Kirkus*

"The news feels so heavy, the future so uncertain; we wonder if we'll ever feel steady again. In this beautiful book, Gillian Deacon reminds us that uncertainty can be a gift—grounding us in humility, awakening us to awe, and showing us that we don't need all the answers to live a courageous life."

—Kate Bowler, *New York Times* bestselling author of *Everything Happens for a Reason*

"This is not a book of health tips, easy fixes, or shortcuts. Instead, it's about a much more important question—in the face of uncertainty, how can we live a good life? Gillian Deacon is a warm, wise, and generous guide as she takes a reader along on her search for answers. *A Love Affair with the Unknown* brims with curiosity, wisdom, and life. It's a balm for our troubled times. I loved it."

—Claire Cameron, author of *How to Survive a Bear Attack*

"Smart, surprising, and often lyrical, *A Love Affair with the Unknown* offers a masterclass in the art and science of grappling with uncertainty. If you live in the world, you should read this book."

—Alex Hutchinson, *New York Times* bestselling author of *The Explorer's Gene*

"Gillian Deacon writes from the 'night side' of life with the reverent crispness, invitation, and daring play of her radio voice—this book is radiant, wise, and enduring."

—Claudia Dey, author of *Daughter*

"*A Love Affair with the Unknown* overflows with curiosity and joy. In a time when so much of our lives is dictated by algorithms, Gillian Deacon celebrates the unique gifts of a human life: We can wonder, and be astounded, and choose hope over fear. The best things are often a surprise, like this wonderful book."

—Elizabeth Renzetti, author of
What She Said: Conversations About Equality

A LOVE AFFAIR WITH THE UNKNOWN

Leaning into the Uncertainty of Modern Life

GILLIAN DEACON

ANANSI

Published in Canada in 2026 and the USA in 2026 by House of Anansi Press Inc.
houseofanansi.com

House of Anansi Press is committed to protecting our natural environment. This book is made of material from well-managed FSC®-certified forests, recycled materials, and other controlled sources.

House of Anansi Press is an eBound Digital Certified Accessible publisher. The ebook version of this book meets stringent accessibility standards and is available to readers with print disabilities..

30 29 28 27 26   2 3 4 5 6

Library and Archives Canada Cataloguing in Publication

Title: A love affair with the unknown : leaning into the uncertainty of modern life / Gillian Deacon.
Names: Deacon, Gillian, author
Description: Includes bibliographical references.
Identifiers: Canadiana (print) 20250255391 | Canadiana (ebook) 2025025669X | ISBN 9781487013783 (softcover) | ISBN 9781487013790 (EPUB)
Subjects: LCSH: Uncertainty—Psychological aspects. | LCSH: Resilience (Personality trait) | LCGFT: Self-help publications.
Classification: LCC BF463.U5 D43 2026 | DDC 153.4—dc23

Cover design: Alysia Shewchuk
Cover image: *Feel the Fear*, by Gillian Deacon
Book design and typesetting: Lucia Kim

House of Anansi Press is grateful for the privilege to work on and create from the Traditional Territory of many Nations, including the Anishinabeg, the Wendat, and the Haudenosaunee, as well as the Treaty Lands of the Mississaugas of the Credit.

With the participation of the Government of Canada
Avec la participation du gouvernement du Canada | Canada

We acknowledge for their financial support of our publishing program the Canada Council for the Arts, the Ontario Arts Council, and the Government of Canada.

Printed and bound in Canada

For Reggie, Harper, and Miles, who lean into uncertainty with glorious creative gusto

Things fall apart; the centre cannot hold …

… Surely some revelation is at hand.

—*William Butler Yeats, "The Second Coming"*

CONTENTS

PROLOGUE

THIS IS NOT A BOOK about health, nor a memoir of suffering. But it does involve a story of both.

In October 2022, I became very unwell. In a matter of a few weeks, on the heels of a devastating global pandemic that crippled almost every aspect of human society, I went from being a healthy, active, fun-loving working mother of three young men to a near-catatonic slug-person, limp as an overcooked noodle. My symptoms have been varied and unpredictable, the trajectory of any recovery seemingly flat.

At some point in recent memory—a specific date less easy to pinpoint—life for nearly everyone became a lot harder to take. Conflict, climate disasters, and insecurity began to escalate, while truth, integrity, and goodwill seemed to dissipate. All this while artificial intelligence threatens to make human existence irrelevant.

In both cases, mine and the world's, symptoms persist; life appears to be permanently altered. Uncertainty is our collective lot.

And given our innate drive to understand—that essential human resolve to strive for progress and solutions—the state of not-knowing-what-is-happening-and-how-to-fix-it is a terribly uncomfortable one. But how else can we approach the unscalable brick wall of a change in circumstance? What are we missing? Could it be that the rush toward certainty is keeping us from something? Something better?

I have spent so much time struggling to find a path through the confusion of this random illness, groping in the dark for solid footing, for guidance on how to move forward. Living for so many months in a body I don't recognize, sick with an apparently undiagnosable illness, I have been trying not to get even sicker with worry. I have lost the ability to work, to engage with the world, to draw sustenance from everyday life.

The only thing that has made sense to me during this wildly complicated time is the attempt to learn how to be okay with not being okay. Illness offers its own lessons on navigating the unfamiliar; insights that illuminate different paths through the unknown. I have read, listened, watched, processed, and digested countless stories and struggles, trying to understand how to sit with uncertainty. Curious as to what I might observe during this unfortunate time, I sat down—on the days when brain, body, and mood permitted—to write. About my own radical undoing, yes, but also about the more universal thoughts and inquiries it has prompted along the way. What lessons could I learn about coping with the unwelcome? What can I summon from others' experiences—and what do I already know myself? Can there be some good to come from this health setback? Might I find something meaningful in this otherwise random stroke of misfortune?

Surely there is a way to equip ourselves to navigate the uncertainties every one of us wakes up to each day, whatever form they take.

By believing that some value can emerge out of so much anguish, I have felt, on some days, more hopeful. As unpleasant as my personal health crisis is, this book is my attempt to render it an opportunity. Writing, as the poet Louise Glück said, "is a kind of revenge against circumstance. Bad luck, loss, pain—if you make something out of it, then you've no longer been bested by these events."

Being sick is a reminder of all human frailty, not just my own. We all, in our own ways, struggle to navigate uncertainty. Illness is deeply humbling and strangely unifying; vulnerability is a common human denominator.

Facing down that vulnerability, expanding our tolerance for ambiguity, is critical to human achievement and every creative act. It is the key to thriving in this wildly unpredictable time in history. Epictetus, the ancient Greek philosopher and an influential teacher of Stoicism, advised that what causes stress is not what actually happens, but rather the attitude we take toward what happens. So I have chosen to take an attitude of connection, using this unplanned upending of my world to explore why we all struggle so stubbornly for resolution and clarity, and what opportunities we are missing by being intolerant of uncertainty. Along the way, I have taken great comfort and encouragement from revising my own relationship with the unknown.

Feeling overwhelmed by these anxious times is an unhelpful response to the inevitability of change. By flipping our view of uncertainty, seeing that mutability of circumstances as liberating—doesn't that make every day a second chance? What if uncertainty could be a motivator to live a meaningful, fulfilled life? If everything can be taken away, then shouldn't we treat all of it like treasure? Precariousness is what makes a circumstance precious. A. R. Ammons put it succinctly in his one-sentence poem "Old Geezer":

> The quickest
> way
> to change
>
> the
> world is
> to
>
> like it
> the
> way it
>
> is.

What I have tried to do in this book is explore how to get more comfortable with uncertainty—ubiquitous and inescapable as it is for us all. There are no bullet points on the pages that follow; no numbered tips or lists of coping tools. You can find enough of that on social media, choked as it is with self-help advice for managing hard times. This is not a quick-fix guide to navigating uncertainty—that sounds suspiciously like a promise of certainty. Rather, it is a reminder that, as Voltaire said, "Doubt is not a pleasant condition, but certainty is absurd." It is a reminder too that, although facing the unknown feels like a lonely condition, we are not alone in going through it.

Uncertainty, syn.: *Uneasiness*

What's the matter here?

An icy tingle buzzes across the top of my head, chilling my scalp.

Rumblings of a sinus flare-up threaten to clog my nose.

It is a warm Wednesday in mid-October. Public health messaging about annual flu shots has begun in earnest. I must be getting a cold—my first since pre-pandemic times. I'd almost forgotten what it feels like.

Normally I might stay in bed for a day or two with brewing symptoms like these, but I have a flight to Vancouver tomorrow, a long-planned visit to see old friends. I pack extra vitamin C and a neti pot, and figure I'll muscle through it.

But I don't.

Through the rest of October and November I continue to work and exercise and carry on with life, but something is ... wrong. Countless COVID-19 tests show negative results.

I feel faint nausea when I eat.

The head chill has intensified—I wear a toque indoors, even to bed.

Why can't I shake this?

I take some time off work, spend four days straight in bed.

I rinse my sinuses with the neti pot twice a day and pour hydrogen peroxide in my ears to ease the discomfort there.

Nothing makes a difference. If this is a virus, it is pernicious and it's starting to piss me off.

I return to work, perplexed, but my stamina is low. Everything is irritating and harder than it used to be.

"Early symptoms of MS."

"How long can a virus last?"

My early December Google search history tells the tale of my growing unease.

Seven weeks after it began, the situation becomes untenable and I take a longer leave from work.

Probably a virus, the doctor opines, and advises rest.

Staying in bed feels too depressing and blurs the structure of night and day, so I set up a daytime rest station on the living room couch. Book, laptop, phone, reading glasses, water. I get up only to make tea or go to the bathroom—a lot of both.

Sinus pain radiates from the centre of my skull, well beyond the reach of any nasal spray. I swallow raw garlic and gargle thrice daily with oil of oregano.

I will defeat you, virus. I can outlast you.

~

The new year is rung in, though not by me. I sleep through the festivities, cruising into January even less clear about what is going on in my body than I was before.

Climbing one flight of stairs leaves me gassed, my leg muscles screaming like they've raced across a finish line.

Wait, what's this? A flirtatious whisper of energy! Some mornings I wake feeling fairly functional; do I dare walk the dog? I do. A wave of relief washes over me, a glimpse of hope that I am on the mend at last. But hours later I am overcome; my body folds in half, utterly depleted. Back to the couch—spent from the most minimal output, and defeated.

I return to the doctor, who orders more tests, including a

thyroid ultrasound to take a look at the nickel-sized bulge on the left side of my throat. (How did I not notice that?)

Doctor Google is not helpful. Over the course of the last three months I have self-diagnosed Lyme disease, sinusitis, candidiasis, hyperthyroidism, type 1 diabetes, and long COVID. They all make sense ... but really they don't. I bide my time between tests and appointments, horizontal and grouchy. Missing life, missing the person I used to be.

I swear I can feel my muscle tissue coming apart after so many weeks of inactivity, the strands of fibre unwinding from one another like those uncoiled springs that go *boing!* in a Wile E. Coyote cartoon after one of his Acme Road Runner–destroying experiments has backfired.

Nothing feels fun anymore. Settling into my seat at a movie theatre has been a lifelong source of joy, but these days I cannot summon the energy to throw on a coat and go to a matinee. Taking a shower and drying my hair is a Herculean feat of human endurance.

Friends offer to pop around for tea and a comforting visit, but the thought of engaging in conversation overwhelms me. I ignore their texts.

My pilot light has gone out. But that is not a recognized medical diagnosis. There is no explanation for what is wrong with me.

And more than anything, that is what I want—that and to feel like my lively, active self again. I want a label for this condition, and the road map for getting through it. I want operating instructions for my body and mind. I want to understand what is happening to me and how soon it will be over. What is this discomfort and for how much longer must I bear it?

When I break down my discomfort, it has two discrete parts: there are the achy limbs and queasy gut, the pounding headaches and ringing ears, yes; but beyond that, and perhaps more problematic, is the feeling of *not knowing*. A wool cap can soothe my chilly head, a long nap will relieve my tired bones, but the uncertainty of my unstable health is harder to ease. *That* is the root of my suffering.

Why does a previously active, high-functioning, healthy middle-aged woman continue to feel like an achy, queasy, wheezy bag of broken parts? What did I do wrong? What could I have done differently?

If I am not able to function as my recognizable self right now, then when?

Will this get worse?

Will I get to cut loose on a dance floor or dash to catch a train or stay up late laughing or sing at the top of my lungs ever again?

I want answers. I need to know that this will pass, and that the world and my ability to navigate it will feel familiar again. But I cannot have that right now. So what do I do when the only solution seems to be lying down and giving up almost everything I have held dear in my life? How long can a person be expected to exist in such a limbic state?

Welcome, the answer appears to be, *to your crash course in uncertainty.*

Buckle up.

BIG UNCERTAIN WORLD

> Somewhere along the line [she] misplaced whatever slight faith she ever had in the social contract, in the meliorative principle, in the whole grand pattern of human endeavor.
>
> —*Joan Didion,* The White Album

WHAT DO WE MEAN by *uncertainty*? For me, in this moment, uncertainty is looking out the window at all the healthy, active people strolling carefree down my street, and wondering how much longer I'll be stuck inside feeling nauseated and wobbly legged from a slow climb up a short flight of stairs. It is wondering what new information the next doctor's appointment will yield; wondering if I'll ever feel better again. But I know I'm not alone in this condition. You don't have to have been struck down by a mysterious malady to identify with the feeling of wanting to hurry up and move through an uncomfortable state of *not knowing*. I would wager that if you draw breath in this moment, you are by default a card-carrying member of the uncertainty club. (Do you wonder about the invisible particulates and toxins contained in that drawn breath? Whether an air quality advisory hangs over your community today?)

Whether you've stopped to identify the source or signature of the agita, it has its fingerprints all over your life.

Perhaps it's that uneasy feeling of wearing a T-shirt in February in Canada.

Or antibiotic-resistant bacteria.

It's the AI technology capable of writing original essays in mere minutes, disrupting the model of education within which societies have operated since the slate tablet. (Maybe that same technology threatens to eliminate the need for your white-collar job.)

The overturning of a woman's right to choose.

Escalating global conflicts that seem perpetually unresolvable.

The unimaginable suffering that intensifies throughout those conflicts, about which you feel gutted, powerless, and unhelpful.

The disquieting rise of paranoid politicians spreading disinformation.

Or the lies being legitimized by people in positions of authority.

The software update you need someone ten years your junior to explain.

Fear of contamination of some of the meat or produce in your refrigerator.

Power outages caused by domestic terrorist attacks on electrical substations.

Wondering if you're doing a bad job with your kids.

Not being able to reach family members in a country ravaged by war.

Hatred and xenophobia, online and in the streets.

The rate of inflation far outpacing any increase in your wages.

Big bills coming due when your projected earnings fall short.

That late-night rabbit hole with Doctor Google, analyzing an unfamiliar twinge or a newfound lump.

Melting permafrost in Siberia, releasing methane, an even more pernicious greenhouse gas than CO_2.

All the avenues of possible outcomes for the angry teenager you want so badly to connect with but whose door is always slammed shut.

Ingredients you can't pronounce.

The lack of affordable housing.

Having to take on a second (or third) job to make ends meet.

Malware attacks on giant institutions whose security you trusted with your personal data.

The spread of avian flu on the heels of a global pandemic from which nothing feels fully recovered.

The collapse of legacy media.

Extremist groups inciting violence.

That text you wish you hadn't sent, or the email hanging in unanswered limbo.

Watching families laughing together in the park on your way to another expensive fertility treatment.

Empty desks at the office because no one wants to commute anymore.

The acidification of the ocean caused by CO_2 in the atmosphere.

Your mother starting to repeat her stories.

Algorithms that hijack your free will.

Learning that because you opted for radiation instead of surgery, there's a 66 percent chance of recurrence for your cancer, and trying to understand why they didn't tell you that earlier.

Shortages on store shelves.

The rash that is spreading.

Corporate layoffs in service of the bottom line.

Watching your young adult child ride their bike in traffic without a helmet, or leave on a road trip with friends whose judgment you're not sure you trust.

Mudslides, earthquakes, wildfires, floods, glacial melts, riverbed droughts, and species decline.

Waking up and bracing yourself for today's news.

Or maybe it's the intersection of all of it, a polycrisis—that is to say, simultaneous calamities interacting and exacerbating one another. The inability to resolve even one of the crises, never mind their compound impact, can lead us to feel absolute overwhelm. Historian and writer Adam Tooze has characterized the current polycrisis as a recipe for sleeplessness, as our minds spin in endless agitation, racing desperately to keep up with the pace of change.

There has always been strife, of course. There has always been famine, flooding, civil unrest, racial discrimination.

There has always been disease and we have long known about global warming. But, historically, we could place a little more faith in a foundation of certainty. In an earlier time, if you were privileged enough to have an education and a job, you could largely count on basic rewards for hard work. The underpinnings of security, as flawed and discriminating as they were for many people, felt generally more stable. Lately those underpinnings have come undone: corporations value profit over loyalty, natural resources are dwindling, social supports are meagre and unsupported, it's every person for themselves. The number of things to be stressed out about has escalated exponentially in the blink of an eye. When did the acceleration of change outpace society's capacity to adapt?

One explanation for the feeling of stepping in front of a fire hose of uncertainty the minute we get out of bed each morning (and sometimes even as we lie in bed, unable to rest) is the disproportion between our ability to *access* information and our ability to *process* it. Computing power has increased a trillionfold since the 1950s; our brains have remained pretty much the same. So one reason for our constant state of overwhelm is the exponential magnification and amplification of information input, augmenting the complexity of literally every situation.

Say your old washing machine breaks. Is it less harmful to the planet to purchase a newer, energy-efficient model that is manufactured offshore and requires the burning of unquantifiable fossil fuels to be transported to your door? Or have the old one repaired locally and for it to continue to guzzle comparatively more water and energy? Ethical debates, scientific research, marketing and sales spin, personal anecdotes, financial implications, political policy—every kind of argument for either choice is at your fingertips. And so it goes, whether it's what to eat for dinner, how to get to work, where to live, whom to vote for, how to raise your teenager, how to spend your free time. No wonder our 1950s-sized brains have us feeling overwhelmed with the uncertainty and perilousness of just about everything. Those powerful pocket-sized computers we carry around rarely give us any real agency in relation to all the calamitous things they alert us to.

But even within the landscape of 24-7 news cycles and constant access to a frantic digital universe, it feels as though there has been a tipping point. Codes of acceptable political conduct are being rewritten before our eyes, journalism and other traditional means of holding those in power to account have been undermined, facts themselves have come into question, and power dynamics have shifted—nearly every day can feel precedent-setting in one way or another. And technology serves it all up to us on a platter: a smorgasbord on which we've begun to gag.

It occurs to me, checking my phone just now to see if those dark clouds outside my window will bring rain this afternoon, that in addition to the seemingly endless barrage of uncertainties we face at this point in human history, there are factors in contemporary life that are constantly at work to undermine our capacity to cope with those uncertainties, deconditioning our ability to handle not knowing.

Technology has bestowed many gifts on the modern world, but being able to control outcomes isn't one of them. Don't get me wrong, I'm as excited as the next person for a new gadget, and I do appreciate the weather app's guidance on what clothing to pack for a trip or a food app's intel on how long to cook a pork tenderloin. But I do often pause to consider that for all its time- and energy-saving benefits, that same technology is dulling the human capacity to adapt. GPS maps on our phones have eroded our sense of navigating our own way, but more importantly I believe they have abraded our comfort with veering off a set path. Think of the last time your navigation software failed you, or your route took significantly longer than the app had anticipated—your response may have been indignation or even outrage at the assault on your plans. The ever-present reality of crowded streets and the infinite possibilities they hold for spontaneous mishaps is overlooked, on the misplaced assumption that the higher power of algorithms should triumph.

It's the same with weather apps; we have conditioned ourselves to believe that knowing the day's weather patterns is our right and our power, an accumulation of oversight that we mistake for control. Such apps have normalized the illusion of predictability of something as patently unpredictable as weather. Pity the poor weather forecaster who is inevitably cursed for having misread the meteorological tea leaves, promising sun and warmth when in fact a rainy chill is in store. An inaccurate forecast on a weather app yields the same reproach. By promising to accurately relay temperature, precipitation, and wind speeds, weather apps are a false prophet; even though they will never be consistently reliable, they offer us the misguided fantasy of certainty. They've also made us stop looking at the sky and smelling the air for clues.

Digital invitations show you the full guest list, so you know in advance who else will be at the party; Netflix previews reveal scenes and characters before you commit to viewing a series; movie trailers have become so detailed in plot as to make watching the entire film practically redundant. Somewhere along the way we surrendered serendipity, that most charming of uncertainties. Every app on our phones that offers a shortcut—weather, navigation, automated parking payment, preselected grocery orders—is also by definition removing some interactions that, tedious as they may be, have historically kept our coping muscles in shape: pausing, reflecting, choosing, evaluating, waiting. By speeding us through the process, technology removes friction; it shaves off layers of the experience of dealing with challenges, and makes us less inclined to want to face them. Apps and gadgets are polished to user-experience perfection, to streamline our interactions, serve our needs, and meet our demands—instantaneously. We're not just addicted to our phones; we've grown addicted to the certainty they promise. Our devices have neutered our ability to navigate choices and challenges, all while duping us into thinking we've got everything under control.

The next time you're sitting in a waiting room or moseying along the aisles of a grocery store—listen. The soundtrack to your retail experience, your haircut, your elevator ride, has likely been preprogrammed by an algorithm that presumes to know what the average consumer might like to hear; what mood-enhancing music might increase our comfort and lead to more purchases. Even our personal listening has become automated; life is busy, who has time to stay up to date on the latest bands and songwriters? So we opt in to curated playlists, letting the algorithm take cues from our previous listening habits and offer up new selections. We might even feel pleased with our expanding repertoire of playlists—an endless stream of agreeable listening at the ready.

But the price of that convenience is the guardrails of taste that those same algorithms put up around us. By staying within these computer-generated parameters, we are never made uncomfortable, never pushed into new sonic spaces—the very places our musical appetite grows and expands. We never experience the uncertainty of something truly new. I wonder if we're losing the taste for it. As American poet laureate Joy Harjo suggests in her memoir *Poet Warrior*, these devices with memory lead to users who forget.

The technology-as-surety model also applies outside of the machines in our pockets. Data models form the basis of economic forecasts and political and business decisions. Analysts track statistics and make predictions; algorithms see patterns and make prognostications. Technology's ability to offer up instantaneous answers to any query has become this century's opiate of mass appeal. And yet somehow, in this information overload of ever-accessible data, it seems that the more we know, the less we understand.

There is no doubt that technology has accelerated our

ability to share and receive evidence of our unstable world, but it is unequivocal that uncertainty and change are—no matter how badly we would like it to be otherwise—constant. In the midst of a rinse-and-repeat cycle of calamity, when there appears to be no cohesive narrative of these times beyond brace-yourself-for-ruin, there is comfort to be found in remembering that uncertainty and change are, in any period of human history, the essence of life. The Polish poet and Nobel laureate Wisława Szymborska, in her 1976 poem "Utopia," imagines an island where everything makes sense, a land of clarity and conviction, where the ground is solid and the wind quickly blows away any doubts and fears. And yet no one lives there. Any visitor to the island inevitably leaves, turns back to the choppy waters of the sea of uncertainty, and dives back in to real life, unfathomable as it is.

Unfathomable life is the reality, yes. With a deep breath to calm ourselves, we can concede that uncertainty is inevitable and part of being alive. In fact, we turn toward it; we need the rich mystery of life's unknowableness. We understand, deep down, that a life that went entirely to plan would be joyless.

And yet it remains equally true that uncertainty makes us nervous, a feeling we instinctively want to reject. The reflex when we feel nervous is to grasp for some kind of control. Instant gratification has made a shambles of our ability to handle confrontation, to manage disagreements, even to endure things simply not going as planned. What's worse, it has eaten away at our powers of empathy. For all our instincts toward it, certainty is the great enemy of tolerance.

Intractable political divides causing tensions worldwide are the result of each side leaning furiously into their own certainties. The "manosphere," as online circles promoting misogyny have been called, is the product of young men feeling uncertain about their future—uncomfortable with, and staunchly resisting, societal shifts toward equality.

Intolerance to discomfort and to different points of view makes us grab with greater and greater desperation at the false promise of order and command. But clinging to certainty makes for a short trip to autocracy. New rules, new policies, new restrictions are almost always a reaction to some degree of uncertainty. They are an impulsive resistance to the discomfort of change, but they can actually make things worse. You cannot manage uncertainty with control. This polycrisis world, this unprecedented level of uncertainty, calls for a whole new way of living, of leading, of learning. And it starts with sitting squarely in our discomfort, and recognizing it for what it is.

These are liminal times: we hover between the beginnings and ends of wars, technological revolutions, climate eras, global pandemics, and cultural transformations. The world feels unstable and the future precarious in so, so many ways. *Liminal* feels like the right word for it—that suspended, transitional, threshold, hovering state. *The point that lies in between what is no longer and what is not yet.* Liminal is a doorway between two rooms; it is a pubescent teenager, all blemishes and awkwardness, caught between childhood and being a grown-up; it is twilight.

We experience liminality all the time: it's the period between a medical test and hearing the results, between the end of final exams and the graduation ceremony, between engagement and marriage; it's the waiting lounge at the airport. Many liminal states are innocuous (a gap year), even charming (early dawn). Merriam-Webster defines *liminal* as "of, relating to, or situated at a sensory threshold: barely perceptible or capable of eliciting a response." Which is to say, we don't always recognize the condition until we're past it. How often do you stop to be aware of something shifting—light, sound, temperature, mood—the moment you pass through a doorway from one room to another?

The best liminal states, you might argue, are those you look back on fondly. *Remember when we got lost on the way to the party and had to ask that weird guy on the side of the road for directions?* That's a funny story, once you've safely arrived. But when you're lost and worried you'll never get to the part of the evening where everything is fun and there is cake—when the idea of looking back on this moment feels impossible to imagine, because the obstacles and fears standing in your way right now are too high to see over, too wide to peek around—being in a liminal state feels like torture.

Uncertainty, syn.: *Disquiet*

Let me try to tell you what I hear right now. Come into my head. Plug your ears though—it's loud in here. A deranged toddler is on the loose in my ear canal, smashing their angry, fleshy little fingers onto all the control panel buttons at once. There's a microscopic demon wielding a shard of flint, scraping its sharp point across a fluorescent light tube that threatens to crack open. An impish intruder leans on the top note of a tinny little keyboard. The tiniest bird is in there, howling for recognition, its yellow beak stuck into a crevice in the apex of my cochlea.

Who invited you assholes in? Sit down and stop your screaming. Stop, stop, please make it stop. What do I do if this high-pitched cacophony never ends?

I cannot find a pitch pipe. In this house full of musicians, one would assume that a person who hears an unceasing note ringing in their ears every minute of every waking hour could successfully locate a pitch pipe to establish which fucking note it is. Our family pitch pipe is probably hanging out somewhere with my childhood locket, the egg poacher I remember buying but not where I chose to store it, and that pink sweatshirt I always liked but haven't seen in years. All things that do not currently want to be found by me.

But I do find the Pocket Pitch app. Of course I do. Why I trust my breath shot through a hole-punched metal disc more than I think I should with a digital pitch generator, I don't know. Why do I even care what pitch my tinnitus is? This must be the first official sign of madness. But if I'm going to carry a squealing interloper around with me, allow it to live rent-free in my inner ears, I'd like to get better acquainted with this sonic companion.

Turns out it is a C sharp. In the highest possible octave. I feel certain it is the same frequency as the colour bars that some stations used to air in the wee hours if you left the television on all night. This exact high-pitched hum was designed to wake you up if you fell asleep on the couch.

It's nearly 2:00 a.m. I've been awoken not by the screech in my ears but by my pounding heart, racing like something bad is about to happen. Being woken from deep rest with such vehement intensity is disorienting—what crisis did I miss? Such is the random rowdiness that is my heart these days. It thumps furiously of its own accord, at odds with my sleeping body. And now we're all up, every bit and piece of me, struggling to make sense of the rambunctious, unreasonable thundering in my chest. Deep breathing and mindful techniques have no sway here. This heart is like a puppy who hears a trainer's command, and considers it briefly with a fiendish look from the corner of an eye, before bounding off to tear apart the furniture. I am left with no choice but to lie awake for hours, waiting until it has shredded all the pillows and finally grows weary enough to collapse, exhausted, in a pile of stray feathers. Only then am I allowed to do the same.

The lower left pocket of my abdomen feels ... weird, almost like a bubble of gas that wants to get out but never succeeds. It doesn't hurt. In fact, it's pleasantly reminiscent of one of pregnancy's few charms; I can almost enjoy the reminder of the pressure I'd feel in my growing belly when one of my babies kicked or stretched out. But then I remember that there is no anticipatory joy of a growing baby in there to explain the sensation, and a gas bubble wouldn't present in the same exact spot for over a week, and I don't like it anymore. I definitely don't like it.

My Apple Watch tells me my blood oxygen level is low. Normal levels are between 96 and 100 percent; pretty much everyone's blood oxygen level hovers in that range. Mine was 86 last week. Yesterday it was 81. My doctor says that doesn't make sense—that's the blood oxygen reading of a dead person. I show her the one-month history in the tracker of my Health app; it shows many, many readings in the low eighties. She sends me for a chest X-ray.

THE CERTAINTY TRAP

> The quest for certainty blocks the search for meaning.
> Uncertainty is the very condition to impel man to
> unfold his powers.
>
> —*Erich Fromm,* Man for Himself

SINCE AS FAR BACK AS 1789, we have been cautioned not to put too much stock in the permanence of anything. In a letter to his friend and fellow electricity enthusiast Jean-Baptiste Le Roy, Benjamin Franklin famously wrote (paraphrasing an even earlier literary reference): "In this world nothing can be said to be certain, except death and taxes." They're still the only things we can count on. What the twenty-first century has added to that short list of certainties is an overload of uncertainty itself.

We try our best to avoid it, but it's always right there waiting for us. But what does the condition of uncertainty really mean? If I burrow into the nature of my mysterious health predicament, or any other anxiety-inducing scenario, what is it about the not-knowing that makes it so unpleasant? Is it the realization that what you thought would or should unfold actually did not? Is it the stubborn refusal of life events to follow the comfortable script you didn't even realize you had written in your head for how it ought to be? Is it the possibility that something bad could happen for which you feel ill-prepared?

Umm, yes and yes. To all of the above. Uncertainty is an unwelcome adjusting of expectations. Those expectations begin in our minds, what David Foster Wallace called our "tiny skull-sized kingdoms, alone at the center of all creation." We wake up each day and begin to tally up things we believe to be true. Shoulder still sore, meeting with Janet, report due tomorrow, coffee then exercise then shower, low on milk, catch the 8:01 train, Thursday is payday, order that new sweater we've had our eye on. Then we overlay our own thoughts with the impressions of others. Can't be late or Janet will think poorly of us, exercise will make us look better in our jeans, and so on. Assumptions, plans, and judgments are our default settings, unconsciously building up a thick layer of expectation about how things should proceed, a safe path to navigate life's chaos. But what if the 8:01 train never comes? We are thrust unhappily into the present moment, until we begin to map out a new series of beliefs and assumptions about how to scramble back onto the conveyor belt of planning and purpose.

When a trapdoor opens beneath our feet and what we thought was solid ground falls away, it's natural and inevitable that we feel rattled. Mostly, we wonder if we can handle what comes next and worry we no longer have control. We instinctively want to get back onto the safe path that will lead us to a place whose geography we have anticipated and planned for. Some imagined and idealized *there* seems much more desirable than *here*, because *here* feels confusing and hard to navigate.

What is happening inside our bodies when we feel the speedy pulse, the jittery flutters of nervous energy, that signal anxiety over what might happen next, and what unforeseen scenario may befall us? When we clock a problem—something we did not anticipate and don't feel we have a plan for—our brain registers the risk stimulus and activates our threat response. In acute cases of stress, like when you're driving and a car swerves into your lane of traffic, the emotional processing centre (the amygdala) sends out a distress signal to the body's central command (the hypothalamus). The hypothalamus then communicates with the rest of the body through the autonomic nervous system, which controls the processes that happen involuntarily, like breathing, blood pressure, heart rate, and digestion. The burst of energy you feel, the surge of adrenaline that fires you up to swerve out of the way of the approaching vehicle, is triggered by the sympathetic nervous system. This is the fight-or-flight response—your heart beats faster, your blood pressure goes up, your muscles tense.

But the same kind of anxious response can be triggered by much less immediate danger than an oncoming car. Fear of the unknown can have the identical effect, which is why longer-term uncertainties and instability can cause a protracted anxious reaction. When a threat cannot be resolved as easily as tacking right to avoid a car crash, high levels of stress hormones build up in the bloodstream, contributing to anxiety and even insomnia. Humans are biologically averse to the unfamiliar.

I once read about a 1970s child psychology experiment, considered a classic in the study of human behaviour, called the Strange Situation. In an attempt to better understand the psychological impact of love and attachment, British psychiatrist John Bowlby designed a simple experiment in which one-year-olds were taken briefly from their mothers and placed into a controlled but uncertain situation: they were left alone with a researcher—a stranger—for a few moments before their mother returned to the room. The children were not harmed nor actively frightened, but their circumstances suddenly became foreign. In the absence of something familiar to attach to, the babies expressed fear and distress. If you're a parent who's ever had to leave a young toddler with a new babysitter, you've conducted your own Strange Situation experiment: without the familiarity of their routine caregiver, even a kindly, well-intentioned stranger is alarming to a small child. That fear and mistrust of the unfamiliar is deeply wired. In spite of constant evidence that stability is always fleeting—that entropy is inevitable—almost all humans seek and crave certainty, against more reasoned expectations.

The ongoing distress of an uncertain world can trigger the same response in the long term; chronic low-level stress keeps the adrenal system fired up and humming. Part of the purpose of the fight-or-flight response to an unwelcome experience is to increase our vigilance when it comes to potential threats in our surroundings. From a survival standpoint, this anxious feedback has a productive purpose—worry about the future triggers us to plan for various potential scenarios. The modern insurance industry has that impulse to thank for its success—indeed, for its very existence. After the Great Fire of London in 1666, when most of the city's homes were destroyed, an early version of home insurance was born: houses that had paid for insurance would be marked with a metal plaque, indicating to firefighters which homes to save first in the event of another fire.

Buying a piece of certainty to offset the risk of any future devastation, hedging bets against the unforeseen—the insurance industry is built upon our basic discomfort with uncertainty. And yet it is an arrangement that grows increasingly untenable; in our climate-changed world, the very idea of insurance is a grand overreach. Our anxious response to many of life's uncertainties has, at its core, a degree of hubris. It is based on presumptuous ideas that we are entitled to health, wealth, and happiness, when in fact those are imagined entitlements, and far from guaranteed.

As humans have evolved, our ability to plan has been critical. We have figured out how to anticipate patterns in nature and not be thwarted when we encounter them, and we have taught our children to do the same. Mythology and fairy tales insist that there is a predictability to the universe, an order in which things should happen—and the heroes are the smart ones who figure the pattern out. Between these biological and cultural influences, we grow up most comfortable when we are able to recognize our circumstances, gather the resources necessary to make a plan for handling them, and then go on to implement that plan. And this is, of course, a general pattern for successful forward momentum. In other words, the extraordinarily high levels of uncertainty in modern life are literally at odds with how we've historically advanced, adapted, and thrived as human beings.

In reading a little bit about the psychology of our intolerance for uncertainty, I stumbled on something critical to understanding this moment in time: research suggests that part of our automatic response to uncertainty is to cross-reference it with memory. Fear is described as an automatic response to stimuli as being imminently threatening; anxiety, by comparison, is described as "an enduring subjective response to having experienced fear." In other words, we identify whether something is negative, positive, or neutral by comparing it to known experiences in our memory—has this caused me to feel fear before?—then we react accordingly.

The COVID-19 pandemic, and the multi-year global health and economic instability it triggered, heightened our sensitivity to uncertainties. The frequency, intensity, and relentlessness of these additional uncertainties—climate change, youth mental health, the AI revolution, take your pick—have continued to create and re-trigger anxious memories in a vicious loop of malaise. The pandemic shifted our ability to process discomfort and sit with it patiently until it resolves. That sustained feeling of isolation and confusion was a two-plus-year waiting period, leaving us with an overactive desire to rush through any other of life's uncertainties so we could get back to some kind of equilibrium. We were like the toddlers left in an unfamiliar room with someone we'd never seen before—only we were stuck there for years. And we wanted out the entire time. People in a state of anticipatory anxiety want the time to go faster, to speed up life to the part where we learn the outcome and achieve resolution. Resolution is where we find comfort—*ahhh*, order restored, a return to stasis. Back to a familiar set of arms to hold us tight. And so we itch for time to quicken, willing away our precious days because the more stable condition we crave feels like it's somewhere around the corner.

Psychologists say the anxiety we feel around not knowing what could happen tomorrow is rooted in our attachment to outcomes. Having evolved the aptitude for planning, we humans have become increasingly invested in the payoff. If we follow the steps that we've been told will lead to health and happiness, we darn well better get to reap the rewards of that effort. Sometimes it seems we're constantly pitching forward, leaning into a time that hasn't happened yet, striving and building toward some future state of satisfaction. Seeking is a motor that keeps most of us going, the forward-looking drive toward an outcome. And there are infinite circumstances in which that momentum is beneficial and bears fruit—look around and you'll see innumerable results of human striving for which you might feel grateful. The trick is not to take an outcome as a given, or view it as something we are due because of our planning and preparation. Or maybe the trick is to recognize that the immediacy of the present holds an equal if not greater value to the shadow of future promise. All the planning we do and the banking on future prospects in some ways amounts to a frantic scramble away from where we are—that rush from *here* to *there*. And yet the less we sit *here*, in the present moment, the less alive we feel. But if we are biologically hardwired to feel uneasy with uncertainty, how can we possibly override the natural impulse to seek control and predictability in order to navigate this fast-changing world?

Knowing everything is not an option—obvious, yes, but it's still helpful to remind ourselves of that fact every so often. As we confront this not knowing, there are two paths we can take: we can cling to our presumed assumptions and fear-based theories—or we can widen our perspective to accommodate more possibilities, and open our minds up to new ideas. The Japanese term for this is *mushin*, which translates to "no-mind" and refers to the acceptance of change. If we let them, uncertain circumstances can encourage us to become more creative, more innovative, better at solving problems. Uncertainty is the birthplace of possibility. Author and biochemist Isaac Asimov is reported to have said that the most exciting phrase in science is not "Eureka!" but rather "That's funny ..." Those words—acknowledging uncertainty—herald new discoveries.

The notion of certainty is, if we're being honest, a trap. Once we've developed the life experience and coping skills to recognize and analyze the world around us, I think we do ourselves a disservice by clinging to the illusion of order. Or by fooling ourselves that we're the ones masterminding the plots of our lives. I would never have written the part in my life script where I'm forced to spend seemingly endless months lying down staring at the ceiling, trying to remember how I ever managed to carry heavy grocery bags—and I never saw it coming. While I want out of this uncertainty and to get back to the comfort of something I recognize as myself, I know that no amount of wishing can make it so. So what should we do with a reality we don't like? Our tendency is to view unanticipated turns of events with trepidation, but I wonder how much easier it would be to handle this uncertainty if we didn't assume that shift was, in fact, unwelcome.

Uncertainty, syn.: *Mystification*

Have I experienced any unexplained weight loss? Not really, no. But I can't eat as much when my stomach hurts, so that kind of explains it, right? Does that count as unexplained? There's no room for that nuance on the questionnaire here in the waiting room at the endoscopy clinic, however. A dozen strangers sit alongside me, hunched over clipboards, completing the same questionnaire: identifying symptoms and reasons for having our innards probed, either from the top or the bottom.

Soon after my name is called and my clipboard is taken, I'm in the fetal position on a gurney, still wearing all my clothes. And my winter boots. I haven't had time to talk to anyone about the nausea I've been feeling, or the indigestion after certain meals. One of the technicians keeps bumping into my toes, which hang slightly over the edge, and I worry she'll get slush on her scrubs. Someone removes my face mask. The slush-stained technician leans over to place an oxygen tube in my nose. From behind me, the anesthetist taps the bony top of my hand, looking for a vein. Before she opens the valve to let the sleeping drugs course through the IV and into my arm, before this endoscopy gets underway and the gastroenterologist runs a scissor-winged camera down my esophagus and into my stomach to look for tumours or fungal overgrowth and to snip samples for biopsy, the doctor wants to know if there is any specific area I'd like her to probe. Actually, there is. *The lower left, just above my pelvis. It feels ... strange.*

When I wake up in the recovery chair it feels like a year later, but I can see from the clock on the wall that only about ten minutes have passed since my procedure began. The gastroenterologist pulls back the curtain and leans in to tell me something. Between my half-drugged brain and her face mask, it's hard to understand what she's saying but it sounds as though everything looked normal. She'll biopsy the tissue she removed and my doctor will update me in a couple of weeks. "Just hold tight and wait," she says before turning and disappearing beyond the powder-blue curtain.

Hold tight to what?

My family doctor is stumped.

Blood tests are normal. ECG looks good. Endoscopy shows nothing.

There is something vaguely unusual on my chest X-ray, a bit of thickening of the sac around my left lung. *Non-specific apical pleural thickening*, to be precise. There is also this cramping, a persistent discomfort in my lower left abdomen. My doctor books me for an abdominal ultrasound. She doesn't seem overly worried, but she does want me to connect with my oncologist. I am a two-time breast cancer survivor; no matter how hard I work to keep that worrisome possibility in perspective, it is a significant detail in my health history that cannot be overlooked.

My oncologist weighs in. A series of CT scans is ordered: chest, abdomen, and head.

Head? I don't ask why.

FEEL THE FEAR

Fear is the cheapest room in the house.
I would like to see you living in better conditions.
—Hafiz, "Your Mother and My Mother"

THERE IS ALMOST NOTHING as captivating as a good magic trick. Watching something that defies gravity, odds, and the basic principles of physics and mathematics happen before our very eyes gives us an infusion of awe that feels incredible. Even knowing that it is an illusion, a well-executed trick can cause a rush of astonishment that titillates both mind and body; it is a flat-out betrayal of expectations that can raise our heart rate in anticipation, and perhaps a little fear, yet it comes at no personal cost to our well-being.

And there is almost no one who captivates audiences with a good magic trick quite like David Blaine. Arguably the most renowned magician of his time, he can make his audience believe that it can't be an illusion—his tricks appear as real as they are inconceivable. Blaine was four years old when he first felt the spark of awe for magic. Standing on a subway platform in Brooklyn with his mother, a nearby busker performing simple pocket magic piqued the young boy's curiosity. A few decades later, his own spectacular skill at sleight of hand would make Blaine a household name. Card tricks performed on the street in front of a dozen or more witnesses tickled our wits, seeming to invert the rules of logic. An old-fashioned illusionist with a modern-day film crew to showcase his feats, Blaine quickly became the new face of magic.

In 1999, when he was buried alive for seven days in a plastic box, he took his game to another, Houdini-esque level: dramatic performance artist. Since that record-breaking feat, Blaine has orchestrated countless stunts, each more high-risk and unimaginable than the one before it. He stood for thirty-five hours straight on a fifty-five-centimetre-wide pillar rising thirty metres in the air above Bryant Park in New York City. He spent forty-four days in self-imposed starvation inside a transparent Plexiglas case, measuring one metre by two metres by two metres, suspended nine metres in the air over the River Thames in London. He has swallowed (and regurgitated) fish, engagement rings, needles, swords, nails, and a frog. He has floated more than seven kilometres above sea level by holding fifty-two colourful helium balloons, like a live-action remake of the animated film *Up*.

Is it ego or something more philosophical that motivates him to undertake such dangerous and attention-grabbing stunts? Blaine is a polarizing figure and has many detractors, but no matter what you think of his inclination for the outrageous, the attitude he brings to his work strikes me as a fascinating perspective on sitting with uncertainty and the fear that is baked into it. Few people have as deep an understanding of fear as Blaine—a knowledge he has acquired by facing down those feelings of dread and carrying out a deep investigation of what they're made of. He pushes his body and mind to the limit, and while it's the spectacle of the needle-through-the-arm kind of physical extremes that attracts the most attention, it's the mental attitude behind his stunts that interests me.

What would go through your mind were you to stand, as Blaine did in March 2023 for the opening of his Las Vegas residency at the Resorts World Theatre, atop a twenty-four-metre platform and prepare to jump? The prospect of falling nine storeys onto a pile of cardboard boxes has to be uncertainty at its most acute, and a good reason to be afraid. *What if I don't land on the target? What if I sever my spine and never move independently again? What if I land on my head and die? What if it hurts? What if I look like a fool and end my career?* The list of things to be afraid of in those unusual and perilously uncertain circumstances is long and, from a comfortable seat safely on the ground, somewhat nauseating to even contemplate. But those don't seem to be Blaine's questions as he stands poised to undertake his dangerous feats. What does he think or believe that allows him to process fear differently? In addition to being a spectacle, a marvellous distraction, a gimmicky illusionist who redefines the limits of possibility, Blaine offers an example—extreme and provocative though it may be—that it is possible to change our relationship with the unknown.

Why do we refer to death as the Great Unknown? We cannot possibly know what it will be like, and we associate the inability to prepare for and master something with a negative feeling. But isn't *this*—all that we are alive for right now—in fact the Great Unknown? This hopefully long stretch of days and nights spooling out before us is utterly unpredictable, and entirely outside our ability to control.

Maybe we need to reframe what we think of the unknown. Other terms in the English language used to describe whatever comes after death are rapturously positive: nirvana, paradise, the Promised Land. Following that optimistic logic, we ought to be more comfortable with the state of unknowing, on whichever side of the veil it comes. Are we perhaps more comfortable with uncertainty than we realize, or give ourselves credit for?

How is the series you're currently binge-watching going to end? What will happen to the heroine in the next episode? If you knew, there would be almost no point in watching. The unknown outcome is the very reason you pay all those monthly streaming service charges: to have a constant supply of uncertainty, ready at all times to be served up for your entertainment. Isn't that why we read novels? To float in suspended reality? To feel alive in the uncertainty of a slowly unfolding plot? To free ourselves of the responsibility of making plans and sticking to agendas and routines? Of course, the stakes are lower when we experience uncertainty through a fictional character in make-believe circumstances.

But it goes beyond books and movies. There are other times in our lives when we see uncertainty less as a cause for anxiety and more as a state of feeling more alive.

Think of all the instances in your life where you not only handled uncertainty but actually embraced it. Where would rollercoaster operators or backcountry ski tours be without the human appetite for a little risk? Travel, surprise parties, blind dates, new jobs—we throw caution to the wind and gamble with outcomes all the time. Sports betting apps have proliferated based on our insatiable appetite for the thrill of a sports match—the uncertainty of those outcomes keeps us on the edge of our seats—and the added appeal of wondering about (and gambling on) the margin of victory, the stats of individual players, and every other possible permutation of the unknowable. We might not call it uncertainty, but that's what it is. It's important to remind ourselves that we all have experience with navigating, and even revelling in, the unknown. So why are we afraid of some uncertainties while others bring a rush of pleasure?

In her book *A Field Guide to Getting Lost*, American author Rebecca Solnit writes, "Leave the door open for the unknown, the door into the dark. That's where the most important things come from, where you yourself came from, and where you will go." She makes a fair point: every human life does begin and end in darkness. And yet so many of us are afraid of the dark—and not just when the lights go out.

If you ask a psychologist, there are five fundamental human fears, from which all other fears are shaped. Those five essential fears are: extinction, mutilation, loss of autonomy, separation, and ego death. Uncertainties that seem terrifying to us—environmental disasters, computers taking over human work and creativity, political turmoil—must appear thus because they threaten our physical or psychological survival. Or so we tell ourselves.

But if you asked a writer who built a literary reputation trading on readers' fears, you'd get another interpretation. As H. P. Lovecraft wrote in 1927: "The oldest and strongest emotion of mankind is fear, and the oldest and strongest kind of fear is fear of the unknown."

Lovecraft was never on my bookshelves; horror and dark fantasy don't appeal to me. But I am fascinated by people who are fans of the genre—and why they would willingly stick both feet into the fire of fictional terror and all the gut-churning, blood-curdling, heart-pounding responses it generates.

In fact, research has suggested there may be some benefit to experiencing full-body fear from a book or a film. Brain-imaging studies have shown that watching a horror movie activates the endocrine system—the release of adrenaline and cortisol that prepares us to take physical action to escape a threat—even though we know the danger isn't real; and for many people, that rush can lead to a boost in mood. The horror-flick high.

But beyond the relative safety of a make-believe movie that scares you, how do you feel about real fear in your real life? I know, it sounds like a stupid question. *I feel fearful, silly.* What I mean is, if I told you that you were going to experience fear in your life tomorrow morning at ten o'clock, how would you feel about that fact? Most of us don't like fear. We recoil in most circumstances that cause pain or unpleasantness of any kind. We seek pleasure and positive experiences, treasure and cling to them; and conversely we try to move through discomfort and negative emotions as quickly as possible. We are, after all, just adult versions of those one-year-olds in a Strange Situation, eager to return to the cozy embrace of the loving parent we've always trusted.

That's why David Blaine intrigues me. He may appear to be a foolhardy daredevil with a death wish, but he has invested great time and effort into teaching himself how to overcome fear. Much like Lovecraft, he views fear as the response to a lack of information. "The best way to combat fear," he told Rick Rubin on an episode of the *Broken Record* podcast, "is with knowledge, making a conscious effort to understand the information at hand. You don't jump into the unknown, you do it step by step."

In the case of his death-defying feats, the way Blaine acquires the knowledge to overcome fear is by practising. He doesn't simply decide to stand on a thirty-metre pillar and see how it goes—it only looks that way to the viewing public. To get himself there, to mitigate his fear, he gives himself as much physical, sensory, and intellectual information as possible in advance.

First, he prepares his body. What the audience hasn't seen him do, but which he has discussed in interviews, is go over elements of these stunts beforehand. Blaine says he spent weeks standing on a flowerpot in the corner of his sixteenth-floor balcony ahead of his tower stand. He slept in a plastic coffin in his friend's living room for increasingly long periods of time. He jumped from six metres, then seven, and so on, teaching himself how to land on a pile of cardboard boxes. He learned to pee in a bag. By gradually acclimating his body to the physical challenges involved in each stunt, he was able to manage what might otherwise have seemed unmanageable. The act of standing way up on a tiny pillar (or being buried alive, or sheathed in ice, or going weeks without eating) remains daring and dangerous, but Blaine has trained his body to believe his own mantra: *We can handle more than we think.* (He has reportedly taught his daughter to turn the water to cold for the last minute of her shower, training her to face her fears slowly, bit by bit.) In other words, we can think of fear differently, not by denying it or ignoring it, but by shifting our vantage point. Blaine rises above his fears and allows them to guide him forward.

What if you could alter your own relationship to fear? You probably don't have plans to float over Nevada hanging from a bunch of balloons anytime soon, but our everyday uncertainties can change shape in the light of Blaine's thinking. Instead of recoiling at the first fearful impulse, we can lean in to investigate the source of that fear—the first step in overcoming it. *What aspect of this uncertainty am I afraid of? And how can I gather knowledge and information to help me understand it better?* Blaine studies his fear the way he studies illusion, misdirection, and cardistry. By boring into it, he breaks it into more manageable parts and suddenly fear's limiting power is somewhat neutered. Instead of succumbing to the fear unquestioningly, he chooses to reach beyond it.

Abraham Maslow was an American psychologist best known for his characterization of human psychological health as boiling down to a series of basic needs. The popular depiction of Maslow's hierarchy of needs takes the shape of a pyramid: the most fundamental needs like shelter, food, and sleep run across the base; above them are safety and security, then love and belonging, then self-esteem and the respect of others; and at the peak of the pyramid is self-actualization. Maslow posited that humans cannot satisfy the higher needs without having the basic underlying needs in place.

It is tempting to assume that this works like a ladder—that once you've got your food, shelter, safety, and love life all worked out, you can move up the pyramid to work on self-esteem and perhaps even self-actualization, as though life were a board game. That's how I always interpreted Maslow's iconic pyramid. But popular science writer and cognitive scientist Scott Barry Kaufman points out that a more accurate understanding of Maslow's research shows a constant vacillation between tending to different needs; the board game is Snakes and Ladders—any number of steps along the way can lead to a crushing setback, threatening our basic requirements of sleep, safety, and love.

In an essay in *Scientific American*, Kaufman explains that Maslow never actually intended his hierarchy of needs to be represented as a pyramid, and that this well-known depiction is in many ways misleading. It's not "like a video game—as though you reach one level and then unlock the next level, never again returning to the 'lower' levels." Instead, we are always going back and forth between levels of need, and life is constant uncertainty. As Maslow himself wrote: "One can choose to go back toward safety or forward toward growth. Growth must be chosen again and again; fear must be overcome again and again."

My own strategy to overcome fear has been to "feel the fear and do it anyway," as the popular saying goes. But I realize now that I have misinterpreted the mantra, focusing only on the second half: *do it anyway*. I have always thought that leaping into action is to fully embrace life; that being impulsive and assuming the posture of confidence is the secret. A fake-it-till-you-make-it approach to being—or at least *appearing* to be—fearless.

I have a long-standing love of jumping off rocks and cliffs. Not the twenty-five-metre stuff of David Blaine spectacles, of course. But a six- or even eight-metre jump into deep water is something to which I will always say (a nervous but determined) yes. A *yes* to experiencing seconds of free fall that are jam-packed with so much exhilaration as to feel like minutes; a *hell, yes* to conquering the pounding heart and ripples of full-body heat telling me to back away from the rock's edge. But I can't listen to that fear. I need to defy it. I need to prove it wrong and show myself that it can't defeat me, limit me, hold me back from that fleeting rush of a carefree plummet. There is nothing more powerful than that fraction of a second when I override what is surely a sensible, evolutionarily sound, protective urge to stay back from the edge—and I leap. I *do it anyway*. Crashing into the safe embrace of the cool water, pointed feet flapping like every baby held over a bathtub, I feel vindicated. And a little bit stronger every time it happens.

For most of my life, I operated on the principle that if I do the things that most people are afraid of, then I must be brave. Striking a devil-may-care pose of bold spunkiness, my audacity speaks for itself. See? I'm doing things that terrify me, therefore I must be fearless and powerful. Diving in as a posture of daring. But I see things differently now; more completely. In my haste to move impulsively into the action that I feared—to *do it anyway*—I was racing past the first half of that boldness directive, the part that matters most: *feel the fear*.

Doing something courageous without reframing how we think about sitting in difficult emotions like fear, pain, and uncertainty is just a flex. Feeling the fear, getting close to it, sitting with it, identifying it, naming it, honouring it, tracing its energetic path through your body—that is the part that makes you strong. Feeling the fear and doing it anyway is a two-step process, and I've only recently come to see how much I've skipped the first step.

The other, perhaps even more critical, aspect of Blaine's training is to cultivate a confident mindset. That's where the real magic happens—in his head. I think this is the life lesson we can all take from the radical stuntman. How has Blaine changed his mental approach to fear and discomfort? He accepts everything the way it is. "You can't fight the force of what is happening," he told Rubin. "Whatever feels frightening about the uncertainties we face, we know that panicking about our inability to handle it never helps. You need to have faith that you can handle it and try to stay calm."

Using the information and knowledge he gathers through his research and practice, Blaine bolsters his faith that he can handle whatever happens. It's a faith that drives everything he does, and a confidence he wants the rest of us to think about. "I believe in the idea that we can all push past what we believe is possible."

On the surface, Blaine's call to confidence might sound like an empty you-can-do-it pep rally platitude. But it is more than a bromide; his conviction that we can all handle more than we think we can is rooted in deeper thought, which for him stems from a profound loss. Blaine was raised by a single mother who died when he was twenty-one. "When my mother was dying, she looked at the beauty in everything. She made death very poetic and beautiful. It was the greatest gift she gave me, she made me not afraid of the unknown."

If we put the *ear* in *fear*, as it were, what stories do we listen to it telling us? Most often they are tales of what we think *might* happen; in other words catastrophizing. Psychologists call that anticipatory anxiety—what's sometimes referred to as "bleeding before you are cut." We fear aging for how much pain it may cause us, both physical and emotional; we fear the AI revolution will take away our jobs and our autonomy; some of us fear crowds, while others fear being alone. Whatever fear cripples you at any given time, if you stop and feel it more clearly, its story will emerge.

In her book *Feel the Fear … and Do It Anyway*, author

Susan Jeffers argues that the ultimate fear at the root of every other fear is "I can't handle it." But how true is that? Can I not handle being sick and lying around feeling pain and discomfort? Actually, I can, because I'm already doing it. My former yoga teacher used to like to remind the class, as we held deep poses for longer periods, not to struggle against whatever discomfort we felt but to make room for it, because it was already here.

Can you really not handle whatever uncertainties cause you discomfort right now? Chances are you're either already handling them, or you're anticipating them, in which case you don't know whether you can handle them because they haven't happened yet. Listen to what story the fear is telling and decide whether it is a reliable narrator. What are you assuming?

You may have heard the quip that breaks down fear as an acronym: *false evidence appearing real.* In a way, it's an annoying riff, because some fears are absolutely based on very real evidence—confronting a wild animal can in fact lead to death, as can that oncoming vehicle that strayed into your lane of traffic. But for less immediate fears, those born of uncertain circumstances, the acronym holds a lot of value: they are much less evidence-based. My fear of remaining in a lethargic state of discomfort for the rest of my life is rooted in my lack of a diagnosis, and therefore the absence of any medical options to restore me to wellness. Tom Petty was right about waiting being the hardest part: it's the part where false evidence can appear real and lead to unnecessary suffering. Your fear of whatever uncertainty has you in its clutches at the moment is likely rooted in a combination of evidence that is cherry-picked from anecdotes and news reports, and stories you're telling yourself about your (in)ability to handle whatever is coming. We need more information to illuminate the way forward, some of which must include reminders of all the hard things we have handled before: to recalibrate one fear it is helpful to call up evidence of previous fears overcome. This mental effort of teasing out our anxieties, as with any exercise, becomes easier the more we do it. It helps us get more comfortable with the feeling of being vulnerable.

Maybe horror film fans have the vulnerability bit figured out: willfully immersing themselves in discomfort, feeling its intensity, and knowing that they will survive it is like a training camp for conquering real-life fears. Each time we confront a fear, some of the uncertainty about it dissipates. That's what Blaine is doing by standing on a flowerpot on his Manhattan balcony. And each time I stand atop a silly height and consider plunging into the deep waters below, it gets easier with every jump. Because I can remind myself of past victories: *I have done this before, I can do it again.*

The pain we cause ourselves by dwelling in a state of fear can be paralyzing. If the fear about the earth's changing climate is all you think about, the effect will be depression and despair; if the fear of your gender non-conforming child's future dominates your interactions, your relationship is sure to be fraught and your behaviour less empathetic than you want to be. Think of the difference between stewing over out-of-control wildfires and soaring temperatures every summertime versus taking action in your home or your community to promote environmental action; of how different it feels to wallow in the fear over an uncertain medical diagnosis than it does to take a walk with a friend. The action doesn't guarantee a different outcome, but it allows for some forward momentum that is positive: a shift in mindset, a step toward a new attitude. Action is the antidote to despair, as Joan Baez once wrote. Taking some responsibility for the source of a fear can help dismantle it.

The 2022 film *Stutz* is a documentary that tells the story of the psychotherapist Phil Stutz, made by surely one of his most famous patients: Jonah Hill. A major divergence from the brand of the Hollywood star best known for bro-comedies like *Superbad* and *21 Jump Street*, it would be reasonable to wonder if Hill might have overreached by attempting a serious film outside his typical genre. But *Stutz* is a brave creative undertaking by an actor with a lot on the line. Unusual in both its subject matter and its telling, the film is about struggle. Struggles with mental health, physical health, family, self-esteem, creative choices, integrity, and even existential struggles. Hill wanted to make a film about the universality of adversity and also to profile his therapist, so that more people could benefit from Stutz's coaching and coping strategies the way he has.

Stutz says there are three inescapable aspects of reality:

pain, uncertainty, and constant work. Not exactly the stuff of bedtime stories, but a notion that is comforting in its own strange way. There is some peace to be found in the acceptance that life is dense with challenges and requires relentless effort.

Hill took the hardest thing in his life, his deeply personal challenge to love and accept himself, as well as other core revelations laid bare in his own therapy sessions, and sat right smack in the middle of it all with the cameras rolling. Out of his incredibly painful personal experiences, he tried to make something creative. As the film unfolds, it becomes clear that when the first-time documentarian came to realize he didn't know whether the whole exercise was working he sat openly with that too. In *Stutz*, both the filmmaker and his subject honour the process of dealing with pain, uncertainty, and hard work. It strikes me as a fine example of feeling the fear. Seeing it for what it is and accepting everything about it. And doing it anyway—having faith that something valuable will come out of adversity.

Extinction. Mutilation. Loss of autonomy. Separation. Ego death. Psychology's distillation of fear to its basic essence checks out for me; strands of each one of those fundamental fears are woven into my state of uncertain health. Will this unknown ailment prove fatal? Might some part of my body need to be removed? Perhaps my ability to walk or leave the house will become increasingly limited, or I'll need to be hospitalized. What if I become so altered from my old self that no one recognizes this languid version of the woman they once knew? What if no one wants to spend time in my dreary, leaden company? Is the person I thought I was gone forever?

It's an interesting exercise; you could try it with whatever anxiety you feel about your uncertain world: drill down into it until you come to the deepest reason for the fear or worry you carry. Really look at it, feel it, let it exist in its entirety. Swiss psychiatrist Carl Jung argued that everything eventually makes way for its opposite. Jung's concept was based on an idea from the ancient Greeks called *enantiodromia*: once something becomes fully itself, it starts to turn into its opposite. The fullness of something leads to its disappearance. By that logic, in facing our fears, sitting with them, and looking them in the eye, we dismantle them.

In his poem "A Community of the Spirit," thirteenth-century poet and mystic Rumi evokes a powerful image of fearful thoughts as a dense mess of thorny vines in which we have become entangled and from which we might, with the right tools, be able to unsnarl ourselves. Examining the roots of those thorny vines, staring down a fear until its individual parts are exposed and understood, is one of those tools.

Most often, unless you're back in that perilous situation with a vehicle racing toward you in the wrong lane, the things we fear don't actually exist yet. Even in that highway scenario, the source of your heart-pounding fear—your own extinction or mutilation—has not, in fact, yet occurred, though it's a much tighter timeline. Fear is adventitious; it is not inherent to our being, it does not live inside us. It comes from an outside source, usually something we can choose how to react to.

In his *Letters from a Stoic*, the ancient Roman philosopher Seneca observes how many of our fears are, in fact, groundless: "We suffer more often in imagination than in reality." In other words, fear has us believing in something we cannot see, something we don't in fact know to be true. But isn't that also the definition of faith? And confidence? Why, you might ask yourself, are you letting the belief that you cannot handle the outcome of a situation triumph over the belief that you can? "What I advise you to do," Seneca continues in his fifth-century letter to Lucilius, "is not to be unhappy before the crisis comes; since it may be that the dangers before which you paled as if they were threatening you, will never come upon you … We are in the habit of exaggerating, or imagining, or anticipating, sorrow."

As Yann Martel writes in *Life of Pi*, "To choose doubt as a philosophy of life is akin to choosing immobility as a means of transportation." I think we can also say that to choose fear as a companion during hard times is akin to wearing a weighted vest instead of a life jacket when you're learning to swim. The goal is to learn to coexist with our fear. To see it clearly for what it is and understand where it comes from. To think of fear as a worried relative—the nervous, hand-wringing cousin who's quick to anticipate disaster. If that prophet of doom has to be along for the ride, I'm choosing to carry it around as a passenger but I will never let it get behind the wheel.

It's a call to courage, really. Facing fears and standing strong in a swirl of change and uncertainty boils down to finding our courage. Of course, on some days it can be easier to summon than on others. And some days we are reminded that summon it we must, and we can. Like the day I was walking in New York City, bludgeoned by late-day exhaustion and the oppressive summer heat, and I passed a sign in a store window that seemed written just for me. *Courage*, it read, *is a love affair with the unknown.*

During the several weeks he spent in isolation for his stunt "Above the Below," those forty-four days in a glass box suspended over the Thames, David Blaine kept a journal. His notes are an account of his physical symptoms—the throbbing head, racing heartbeat, dry mouth. As his body ran out of enough energy to lift a pen, the entries dwindle to a nearly illegible chicken scratch. But before they do, he documents some of the metaphysical aspects of his experience. In spite of being the target of a lot of anti-American sentiment from Brits on the ground below, who pelted his see-through box with everything from eggs to golf balls and taunted his escalating hunger with barbecued hamburgers, the magician put that negativity in perspective. "In truth, though, none of it really gets to me too much. Just sometimes. But there has been so much peace and love here it negates all else."

Blaine has said that he cherishes the memory of that stunt more than almost any other—when he was able to watch the sun rise and set in minute-to-minute detail. In an inspired act of choosing what to pay attention to, as his body underwent unimaginable discomfort, he journaled that this was a "discovery of how strong we all are in mind, body and spirit."

So, how do we want to spend our days in these wildly uncertain times? Do we want to live and die in fear? Or do we want to face the evidence before us, take action to mitigate our own role in the problem, and make conscious choices about what we pay attention to along the way?

Uncertainty, syn.: *Misgiving*

For weeks I have struggled to complete the daily Wordle—five-letter words are too taxing to conjure; a headache arrives more reliably than the riddle's solution. I used to be good at word games; a quick brainteaser was normally a fun midday mental stretch. I can't remember what normal feels like anymore. Not "normal" by some external standard (the idea that there's a boilerplate way to exist in the world has always struck me as silly), but normal to me. Familiar. Routine. What did that even feel like?

On those days when nothing to do with health or wellness registered on my radar and I had the great good fortune to be mindlessly noodling around with wordplay games, or focused on exciting ideas or boring tasks, how did my body move through the world? How did I experience breathing without a pepper grinder cranking fresh sizzle into my nasal passages, or rubber cement clogging my deepest sinuses? How often was I hungry? What was it like to hear silence?

It has been so long since I felt like myself, it might be time to accept that my "self" was only ever a concept. With every passing day of breathing spicy puffs of ticklish air through my nostrils, walking on leaden pipes, waiting apprehensively for another wave of nausea after eating, listening to cicadas on acid screaming in my head, any sense of my true self as an active, productive, purposeful, engaged member of society feels more and more like a memory than a truth. I like the idea of who I was, I liked that self. I miss her.

I am over this. Over it, I tell you. Who am I to think I know a damn thing about how to manage uncertainty?

Today I got the Wordle in three for the first time in weeks. The answer was WORRY.

WHAT ARE WE PAYING ATTENTION TO?

To pay attention, this is our endless and proper work.
—*Mary Oliver, "Yes, No"*

I'VE OFTEN WONDERED HOW Salman Rushdie gets out of bed in the morning.

In February 1989, a few months after the publication of Rushdie's novel *The Satanic Verses*, Ayatollah Khomeini, then Supreme Leader of Iran, declared a fatwa against the Indian-born British American author—a call for his death. The book, certain Muslims felt, was a blasphemous attack on Islam, for which crime the writer should pay with his life. For a decade following the murderous decree, arguably one of the most notorious terrorist threats of all time, Rushdie lived like a fugitive, in hiding in London, surrounded by police protection. But then, at the dawn of a new millennium, he ventured back out into the world. He moved to New York, published more books, and lived a high-profile life out in the open. Any hope that new Iranian leadership and the passage of time had erased the need for fear was of course dashed in August 2022, when Rushdie was viciously stabbed on stage at a speaking event, an attack that cost him an eye and very nearly his life. A few nights before it happened, Rushdie had told the *New Yorker* magazine he'd had a nightmare in which he was attacked by a gladiator figure holding a sharp object. And yet he persevered with his plans, with his speaking tour, with his life.

What kind of mental exercises did Rushdie have to undertake before heading out of the door in all those years between the invoking of the fatwa and the attack that nearly realized it? What did he tell himself each time he stepped up onto a public stage or into a crowded subway car? How does a person embrace their day-to-day life knowing that their called-for demise could be meted out at any minute? There is, as he wrote in his third-person memoir *Joseph Anton*, no such thing as absolute security. Only varying degrees of uncertainty. And a person has to learn to live with that.

Learning to live with varying degrees of uncertainty—isn't that what we're all working to achieve? Isn't that why you're reading this book? It's certainly why I'm writing it.

Does Rushdie perform some kind of mindset calibrations to frame each uncertain day? Though he remains deeply private about the emotional toll the fatwa has taken on his personal life, it would seem, by virtue of his prolific output, that at least part of his coping strategy has been to invest his energies into the work he loves. He decided, he told the *New Yorker*, to pay attention to how the threat to his life would impact his creative freedom: "I just thought, There are various ways in which this event can destroy me as an artist." Rushdie's intellectual curiosity and hunger for storytelling are where he chose to direct his attention.

Rushdie surely remains acutely aware of the possibility of his imminent death, of the very real prospect that today may be his last. But isn't that uncertainty, as his avatar suggests in *Joseph Anton*, universal? You don't have to be famous or in trouble with the Iranian regime to live each day at the mercy of the fates. Many years ago, walking her dog on a city sidewalk while waiting for snow tires to be installed on her car, my neighbour Evelyn was killed by a distracted driver. Texting behind the wheel, someone lost control and drove into a street light, which fell and killed Evelyn instantly. You don't know the gentle, kind-hearted woman I'm calling Evelyn, nor the three young boys who have grown up motherless, but you will know the ragged, gaping hole left in a different community by some other senseless, unforeseen loss. Every one of us knows of someone whose life ended in a wildly unpredictable and tragic way. Uncertainty about how many days remain is inherent in the life every one of us leads.

Maybe the reason Rushdie's death warrant holds such horrified fascination for so many is that it is an exaggeration and acceleration of the same fate that awaits us all. No matter how dissimilar our circumstances are to those of this internationally recognized, prize-winning author, his uncertainty resonates because it is also our own.

So if that uncertainty is fundamental to being alive, doesn't it behoove us to treat every day as precious? If the future of our planet is deeply uncertain, doesn't it make sense to cherish what natural wonder remains? If, as Susan Sontag wrote in *Illness as Metaphor*, we are all dual citizens of the kingdoms of health and of illness, maybe the trick is to relish the days we live in relative wellness and not clog them with worry about what could befall us tomorrow. Why is that simple attitude of presence *here* so hard to practise?

If technology has removed a lot of the pesky demands on our attention for things like planning a route through traffic or selecting which music we want to listen to, then what *are* we paying attention to? Attention, as Amishi P. Jha writes in her bestselling book *Peak Mind*, is the flashlight that selects and directs our brainpower to process and respond to a smaller subset of information, narrowed down from a wider sea of stimuli. In the seemingly endless stretch of fog I find myself wandering through as a person who is unwell and unclear about why, I am trying to be more aware of where I choose to shine that flashlight beam. We are always paying attention to *something*, but how often do we stop to examine what it is and whether we might adjust our view and point the flashlight elsewhere? Could the subject of our focus have an impact on how we perceive and manage the distress of being unsettled, and how we respond to the unforeseen?

In short, the answer is yes. What we pay attention to, and how much credit we accord it, has a direct impact on how we handle change and uncertainty. Psychology researchers call this attention bias—the human tendency to lean into negative stimuli and be triggered by them more than by other, less worrisome events. Without realizing it, we are quite selective in what we notice. Do we keep track of a colleague or lover's shortcomings and missteps with a sharper eye than we catalogue their good qualities? Do we register only the dangerous applications of artificial intelligence, and undervalue the beneficial ones? Do you react more strongly to stories of climate disaster than you do to examples of innovative solutions? Do I clock the days of painful, debilitating symptoms more reliably than the ones when I have some spring in my step? Evolution has taught us to ignore existential threats at our peril, so in a sense we start off at a disadvantage—humans are hardwired for that cognitive bias toward negative information.

Researchers in France compared the responses in a group of healthy individuals to a series of scenes put in front of them; some of the scenes featured negative details, and others were made up of more neutral images. But in addition to asking the subjects to analyze their responses to what they were looking at, the researchers looked directly at what, exactly, the subjects saw—tracking where their eyes landed. By tracking both eye movement and mood, the researchers found that negative information held people's attention for significantly longer than neutral stimuli once it was fixated upon. Participants who identified as more anxious were most likely to remain fixated on the negative stimuli for longer. This suggests that if we start out anxious, we'll find evidence in our circumstances to validate and perhaps even amplify that distress.

In that "enduring subjective response to having experienced fear"—the clinical definition of anxiety—the brain often takes shortcuts in what it tracks and analyzes, in order (it reasons) to keep us safe. When we are in an anxious state, we make assumptions about what we should be paying attention to; we establish a mental shorthand for what deserves our concern—we operate by rule of thumb. The phrase *rule of thumb* originates in an early English idea of using the width of a thumb as an approximate unit of measurement: its size presumed to be roughly equivalent to an inch. But it doesn't take much thought for that rule to break down. Whose thumb would that be, exactly? And what if I don't have a seventeenth-century English male's thumb handy? Measuring with a part of the human body is at least as inexact as it is convenient. As a rule of thumb, the ice on the lake should be frozen by this time of year ... would you snowshoe very far offshore based on that? Shorthand assumptions leave a lot of room for error.

For such a highly regarded complex organ, the human brain actually makes faulty assumptions a lot, and not just when we find ourselves in a state of heightened anxiety. One of the most famous examples of the brain's impulse to take an erroneous shortcut is something called the Checker-Shadow Illusion, an optical trick published in 1995 by Edward H. Adelson, professor of vision science at the Massachusetts Institute of Technology. Perhaps you've seen it: a 3-D image of a black-and-white checkerboard, with a green cylinder positioned in the top right corner casting a shadow across the board. The brainteaser question is to decide which of two marked squares on the board is darker in colour—square A (not in shadow) or square B (within the shadow). It looks for all the world as though A is darker than B. But in fact, when the two squares are separated out from the larger image and viewed side by side, they are an identical shade of grey. Why are we fooled by the squares in the image? Because a shadow makes things darker, that much we feel sure of, so square B must be lighter than it appears. The brain misinterprets visual cues and runs a quick shortcut to make an erroneous analysis. Even after learning that the two squares are identical in colour, the brain will persist in its error. Unable to stop paying attention to the presence of the shadow cast by the cylinder, it makes the leap and assumes that one of the squares must be a darker colour.

The brain's habit of taking shortcuts and being selective in what it processes is a growing field of psychological study, and a big reason why eyewitness testimony is considered unreliable as a basis for judgment in a courtroom. There are simply too many cognitive biases and other factors getting in the way of the brain's ability to observe and interpret events precisely. Conduct your own anecdotal experiment about who saw what in a film clip (or who said what to whom at dinner last Thanksgiving), and you'll see how often our awareness of what is happening is inaccurate.

What other things are we paying attention to that are not giving us an accurate sense of what is true? In the case of the long list of factors that feel destabilizing—the elements of modern life that contribute to our discomfort—it's worth pausing to reflect on how often we notice something that might echo a past fear and automatically activate a stress response, even though it doesn't pose a direct threat. Such shortcuts are not always helpful or truthful. Given that we suffer, social scientists tell us, from the illusion of validity, in which we continuously overestimate the accuracy of our own perceptions, it is both prudent and beneficial to be aware of our own fallibility.

A popular analogy from Indian philosophy points out that a person walking into a dark room can easily mistake a coiled rope for a snake—a reminder that things aren't always what they appear to be. Many of us pay too much attention to threats, be they real or imagined. *This thing is inherently dangerous or problematic, therefore I should feel fear and concern.* We can also tend toward a kind of appraisal bias, in which we not only overestimate the threat of some kind of negative stimuli but also habitually underestimate our potential to cope with it. And there it is again, the deepest and most fundamental fear: our inability to cope with or handle what change may come. As a result of our appraisal bias, we force ourselves to experience negative emotions more frequently than is warranted. Seneca was not wrong about us suffering more often in imagination than in reality. But why, it bears asking, suffer twice?

Standing at a downtown intersection the other day awaiting the pedestrian cross signal, I watched a driver swerve into the other lane and screech through the light as it turned red, having grown tired of waiting for the taxi in front of him to turn left and get out of the way. His speed, his impatience, and his reckless driving made those of us standing at the intersection shake our heads in disbelief. "What is the world coming to?" the man beside me muttered, throwing up his hands. "People are getting more and more crazy."

It was easy to heave a disheartened sigh and continue on my way, a little more discouraged than before about the declining state of our world order. But would that be accurate?

It's a familiar refrain: society is falling to ruin. Things aren't what they used to be, right? It's what we often tell ourselves. An undercurrent of the uncertainty we feel about the state of the world is the gradual erosion of basic respect and compassion between human beings, yet there is compelling evidence to show that notion is factually incorrect. And it's the result of a type of attention bias.

Goodness knows it has been a successful political strategy to capitalize on that belief: to offer the illusion of being able to stall progress, put the genie of change back in the bottle and restore old-fashioned values. To make America, as a certain political slogan goes, great again. Donald Trump, like Hitler and other demagogues before him (and like many other populist, fear-based political movements on the rise around the world today), appealed to the electorate's discomfort with uncertainty and used that widely felt angst about the decline of human decency to make them vote for the security and harmony he promised. But, never mind the utter fallacy of the MAGA slogan's promise, the notion that society is falling to ruin is absolutely untrue.

Harvard cognitive scientist and psychology professor Steven Pinker argues in *Enlightenment Now: The Case for Reason, Science, Humanism, and Progress* that by nearly every metric—things like life expectancy, maternal and infant mortality, prosperity, safety, violence against women, literacy and education, global democracies, and human rights—the world is in fact getting better, and that we are living in the most peaceful time in human history. You wouldn't think so, based on the typical news coverage, but the historical data bears it out. Yet, in spite of being lucky enough to be born at such a prosperous point in human history, we remain inclined to catastrophize and assume the worst about the state of our world.

In his blog *Experimental History*, experimental psychologist Adam Mastroianni breaks down a paper he co-authored in the journal *Nature* entitled "The Illusion of Moral Decline." His research shows a couple of noteworthy things: first, that people have lamented the *idea* of a decline of human decency since surveys on the subject began in 1949; and second, that respondents' answers regarding lived experiences have remained steady. Questions such as "Were you treated with respect all day yesterday?" and "How much do you volunteer with a charitable cause?" and "How much incivility do you experience at work?" were answered consistently favourably over a twenty-year period by more than 12 million respondents in 140 surveys. Cooperation rates between strangers have in fact increased over time.

Yet the same respondents also assumed that society's overall grace was in a state of decline, even though that assumption differed from their own experience. How does that happen? You guessed it: we pay more attention to negative experiences and information about others. And that attention bias combines with memory bias, in which we remember things as being better than they were. The combination of these two neurological fallibilities leads us to believe in some sort of golden age that has passed, and to feel a misplaced longing for the good old days that in truth were much the same as these days right in front of us—and in many ways, much worse.

It's a depressing thought to dwell on, the idea that we're all going to hell in a handbasket, but it becomes silly when we realize it's not even true. One of the most common symptoms of depression is the tendency to attend to negative stimuli in the world and negative thoughts in the mind. So our impulse to assume the worst about things that happen outside of our expectations or presumption of order is not only inaccurate, it also has the power to lead us down a dark path. Our tendency to take mental shortcuts and make assumptions keeps us stuck in negative feelings about whatever uncertainties present themselves. Even worse, it stunts our ability to solve problems or readjust to changing times.

Living in an uncertain world, one thing is certain: the best skill with which we can arm ourselves is adaptability. But if we interpret every unforeseen shift as a threat, we'll be too busy resisting to be able to grow into the strength we need to handle that change.

~

Let's take a few minutes and go for a walk. I don't have the energy to undertake anything ambitious, but this outing doesn't require hiking boots; there's no uneven terrain. We can do it in ordinary shoes, wherever we are. We're going to walk around a bit and try to summon awe. Yes, awe—that transcendent feeling of being so captivated by something outside of ourselves that we are relieved of our troubles, even fleetingly. We tend to think of awe as something that requires great might or spectacle: like seeing a rhinoceros up close or catching the rare light show of the aurora borealis. But awe happens in quieter moments too—and the more we seek it, the easier it becomes to summon. Birdsong can do it for some; for me it's the patterns in tree bark, and the fractals of branches set against a backdrop of sky; we're sure to find something on our outing.

I've been reading about "awe walks," a cutesy name for allowing a sense of wonder into our minds. Awe is, I believe, all around us to be appreciated at any time, but it only presents itself to minds that are curious and open. We spend most of the day focusing our attention on striving, hearing the siren call of *there*, so it's easy to hurry past the buffet of awe spread out right *here* in front of us.

Try it for a minute here on our walk. Feel the temperature of the air on your skin, the same air that surrounds everything you see around you, sending unseen signals to the plants and trees about what comes next. Listen to the soprano squeals of the children careening madly on a swing set—your voice used to sound like that, back when you didn't worry so much. Look at the kindly expression on the crossing guard's face as they usher us through stopped traffic—their friendliness, indifferent to the glowering looks from impatient drivers all around them, is infectious, if we let it be. Smell that waft of lilac in the air; lean in and stick your nose into that pale purple bloom to inhale it deeply.

Yes, stop and smell the flowers. It is, indeed, awesome. There is a degree of awe and enchantment to be found in the most ordinary of scenes. We have only to remember to shine the flashlight and look for it.

Have you ever found yourself mindlessly caught up in a habitual task, or ruminating on something you did or forgot to do, your thoughts like a conga line of nagging concerns—each more importunate than the next—when all at once you hear the sound of birds overhead? Whatever you're in the midst of, when you pause to listen for birdsong, suddenly it's there. But of course, it has been there all along. Why would we willingly choose to miss the sweet warbling call of a song sparrow or the imperious squawk of a blue jay, and instead hear only the clamorous horns of anxiety and the constant call of our to-do list? And yet we do. How many times have you found yourself in a beautiful corner of nature with lousy cell reception, and spent an embarrassing amount of your precious time struggling to get online instead of being present right where you are and paying attention to whatever is in front of you? Billions of tech industry dollars have been invested in monopolizing our attention, in designing algorithms to steer it constantly back to our devices and their bottomless cavern of exigencies. In our culture of urgency, with the constant demand of texts and alerts keeping our brains in high-alert, fight-or-flight mode, being a first-class noticer is hard. Being in charge of where we direct our attention is a simple skill, but it is one that requires regular practice to master. Perhaps we should take these awe walks more often.

Long before *Silent Spring*—the earth's siren call that became her most famous opus—the great Rachel Carson wrote an article in a 1956 edition of *Woman's Home Companion* magazine extolling the virtues of teaching children to notice the magic and wonder of nature. "For most of us, knowledge of our world comes mostly through sight, yet we look about with such unseeing eyes that we are partially blind. One way to open your eyes to unnoticed beauty is to ask yourself, 'What if I had never seen this before?'" Helping a child to learn to appreciate the endless fascination of the natural world can, said Carson, lay the groundwork for a lifelong openness to awe. But we don't have to be children to be childlike in our wonder about what is happening all around us. We grown-ups just have to recognize the value in doing it, and put down our devices long enough to feel the deep and abiding pleasure of surrendering to a little awe.

Fred Rogers, an icon of comfort and encouragement for generations of children who watched his *Mister Rogers' Neighborhood* public television program, which aired from 1968 until 2001, once told Charlie Rose in a televised interview, "I'm concerned our society is much more interested in information than wonder. How do we make time for reflection? Oh my, this is a noisy world." Awe and wonder always turn down the volume on the clamor.

Awe can of course also be a part of something darker, a more frightening escape from present reality: "shock and awe" was the US military's catchphrase for the American invasion of Iraq, after all. That's a bastardization of a beautiful system—the human capacity to feel reverence for something bigger than our small selves. But for the purposes of helping ourselves sit in uncertainty, considering terror and destruction as awesome forces makes no sense; I will always choose benevolent sources of amazement. In fact, looking up right now as I type, I behold a shimmering light show, a flickering dance of brightness and shadow playing out in front of me—the morning sunlight, filtered through leafy branches blowing in the breeze outside the window, is screening a short art film on the back of a chair. After a few minutes, shadow fills the space and the moment of grace has passed. But the lift I felt in my heart remains. There it is, waving at me across this small room. The lasting gift of awe.

Why does something so simple, so ubiquitous, so easily accessible as a pattern of light and shadow have such a profound impact on me? And not only on my mood—the muscles in my neck and stomach have come unclenched; my whole body feels more relaxed. I am not, in this moment, a feeble-bodied woman with a chronic headache and no ability to plan for the future; sitting in awe, I am transported. All is well, and I am enough just the way I am. But how does this magic work?

Awe is an emotional response to a transcendent event. What feels transcendent can be different for each of us: beautiful art, intellectual epiphany, natural wonders, extraordinary feats of human accomplishment can all evoke the intense emotional response of awe. It turns out that being in a state of awe activates a web of neural pathways around the spinal cord that slows the heart rate and deepens our breathing. Brain imaging studies show that experiencing awe reduces the activation of our self-referential default neural network—awe gets us out of our own self-obsessed heads, makes us more open-hearted and curious-minded. In awe, we are literally humbled.

Studies demonstrate that feeling awe increases generosity, ethical decision-making, and prosocial values, and decreases entitlement. Research cited in *Psychological Science* shows that people who experience awe feel less stressed about time and generally less impatient, due to "awe's ability to alter the subjective experience of time. Experiences of awe bring people into the present moment, and being in the present moment underlies awe's capacity to adjust time perception, influence decisions, and make life feel more satisfying than it would otherwise."

In his book *Awe: The Transformative Power of Everyday Wonder*, Dacher Keltner defines his title subject as the feeling of being in the presence of something vast that transcends your current understanding of the world. In fact, Keltner—a long-time psychology professor at the University of California, Berkeley, and head of the Berkeley Greater Good Science Center—argues that discovering awe can be a direct pipeline to happiness. And he makes a point of debunking the argument that awe comes with a price tag. If the idea of stopping to smell the roses, and inhaling the awe of such a heady perfume emitting from a thorny garden bush, feels like the purview of the privileged, a flight of fancy that those of us too busy trying to put out fires and feed our families could ever have time for, then the act of experiencing awe is misunderstood. It doesn't have to come from a rarified, exotic experience; Keltner argues that awe is available to us all. He interviewed prisoners in San Quentin prison who described their own experiences with awe, finding it through holding the hand of a grandchild, watching passing clouds overhead, reading the Qur'an, or listening to music. Awe, Keltner says, is almost always nearby, and is a pathway to healing and growing in the face of the losses and traumas that are part of life.

British author G. K. Chesterton once wrote, "I am not absentminded. It is the presence of mind that makes me unaware of everything else." A helpful strategy, indeed. Having the presence of mind to observe and appreciate simple, awe-inducing things can lead us down a path that is free of theoretical anxieties and instead lined with the comforting cushion of immediate truth, evidence of eternal cycles and patterns that dwarf our restless worries. Filling your cup with a little awe is a gift—a present of presence, even—that you can choose to give yourself anytime, anywhere.

I find the practice becomes self-fulfilling, as exercise was for me back when my body was healthy enough to allow for it: the more you do it, the more you want to do it, because it feels so good. I also feel certain that the more I seek out moments of grace and awe, the more easily I'm able to notice them even without looking.

I recently took part in an online workshop about neuroplasticity. At one point, we were shown a photograph and told we had ten seconds to study it and find all the things that were red. When the image was taken off the screen, we easily listed the red items: telephone, book on the shelf, the flower on someone's T-shirt, the bowl on the table. Then, without getting another look at the image, we were asked to recall things in the picture that were blue. Not one of us could name a single blue anything. In this exercise, our brains had screened out anything that wasn't red, in a process psychologists call selective filtering.

What are we unconsciously filtering out of our world view every day? If you know (or are) a negative person who is prone to seeing the glass half empty—or red, as the case may be—you've observed selective filtering in action. We often don't know we're doing it, but we can also teach ourselves to do it consciously. As psychiatrist Norman Doidge explains in his book *The Brain That Changes Itself*, humans are capable of training our minds to notice certain things more than others. Your brain gets better at doing whatever you *choose* to do.

Since the common human impulse is to pay attention to the bad stuff, it's no wonder catastrophe, fear, and disorder dominate the news—after all, that's what most compels the human eyeballs and attracts clicks. This means there *seems* to be more bad stuff happening in the world than good, in part because of the prevalence of negative media coverage. Researchers studied the types of words used in written news headlines from 2000 to 2019 and found a consistent increase in those denoting anger, fear, disgust, and sadness; conversely, they found a decrease in what they called emotionally neutral headlines. It is alarmingly easy to buy into the inaccurate narrative that the world is more perilous than ever before; in fact, billions of media dollars are spent on making us believe it. Breaking news alerts on your phone might make you *think* you're being a responsible, informed citizen, but they're not designed to spur you to action—they're designed to keep you subscribed.

With ever-increasing competition for consumers' attention, commercial media outlets have adapted to follow the money: doom = ratings = money in the bank. Algorithms ensure that our social media feeds are populated by stories that keep us clicking, generating more ad revenue for the platforms that host them. All of which adds up to a steady stream of not-always-reliable input and a proliferation of chatter and frenetic opinion-mongering coming at us at warp speed. There's an idea that we must tune into the news to get our bearings in the moment, but in the era of the twenty-four-hour news cycle and endless doomscrolling through hype and calamity, our consumption of the news is having a distorting effect, throwing us off balance. This makes it easy for our attention to be hijacked by distressing narratives, and it's all the more critical that we be conscious of what we are paying attention to.

We can, I am coming to realize as I sit in a stew of aches and pains and an ambiguous future, take conscious control over our thoughts and resist the impulse to grow attached to the ones that make us feel anxious and threatened. As the old story goes, there are two wolves in our inner forest, the good and the bad. The good wolf represents all the things we want to be—honest, courageous, generous of spirit; the bad wolf represents greed, hatred, arrogance, and fear. Which wolf will survive? Whichever one you feed. Humans have a limited cognitive scope; a finite capacity for attention. We get to decide what to focus on in a given moment.

I had a massage the other day. Hoping that the benefits of deep tissue adjustment, some acupuncture needles, and an hour of lying undisturbed on a soft table would assist my recovery, I settled in to relax and enjoy. And I did—at first. I felt the glorious release in my muscles with the pressure of the therapist's firm hands on my stiff joints; I inhaled the aromatherapy of the scented oils; I let the gentle notes streaming from the nearby CD player soothe me.

Then I heard the jackhammers.

I had barely noticed, in my haste to get to my appointment on time, that the street right outside the massage clinic was being torn up. Now, prostrate on a table in the front room of the building, with a single-pane window the only thing between my deep relaxation and the city's construction crew, I was hearing it loud and clear. I felt a flurry of stress-induced responses: frustration, anger, anxiety, irritation. I had come for relaxation, to slip into a deep trance of peace and quiet and serenity. Was I paying a hundred bucks for nothing?

But wait, I thought. *Which one of these things is true? Am I super-relaxed and enjoying the blissful sensations of physical relief from this massage? Or am I lying next to a full-scale construction site, being assaulted by its racket and feeling its vibrations?* Of course, both were true, but I realized in that moment that I had a choice: which was I going to pay attention to?

"The greatest weapon against stress is our ability to choose one thought over another." I've heard that tidbit of wisdom tossed about over the years, but only recently took the time to learn its origins. It is a quotation from the writings of William James, who is often referred to as the father of American psychology. The older brother of the celebrated nineteenth-century writer Henry James, William was blessed with every educational and cultural opportunity, including graduating from Harvard Medical School. In an attempt to better understand his own battle with depression, he directed his medical studies specifically toward human psychology and the idea of resilience.

"The art of being wise," James wrote, "is the art of knowing what to overlook." He was a believer in indeterminism, the school of philosophy that argues that in any situation there is always some degree of possibility not necessarily dictated by the rest of reality—the constant presence of *chance*. James believed that we have agency in our choices, the free will to decide what to do and how to feel about a given situation.

I didn't know about James or indeterminism as I lay on the massage table that day. But it was patently obvious that by dwelling on the unpleasant interruption to the solitude of my relaxation time, I would lose any possible benefit from the experience. Resisting the reality of the benefit that was happening, and dwelling on the irritation instead, would only cause me to suffer. So, I chose relief. I opted to pay attention to the comfort and pleasure of the muscular release, and not the intense cacophony of the urban disruption out the window. The external noise was still there, but its impact on my experience was negligible.

Speaking at a commencement address at Vassar College a few years before she died, the writer Susan Sontag said, "Attention is vitality. It connects you with others. It makes you eager." By that measure, our attention is a precious commodity, something not to be squandered on as-yet-unrealized fears but rather carefully aimed in a direction that gives us purpose and meaning.

"One thing I feel, well, proud of, let's say," Salman Rushdie told *The Guardian* in 2021, "is if you knew nothing about my life, if all you had were my books, I don't think you would feel that something traumatic happened to me in 1989. I'm glad I had the brains to think in the middle of all that: I don't want to be the victim of this. I could write frightened or revenge books, and both would make me a creature of the event. So I thought: be the writer that you want to be."

With what he has described as much determination, Rushdie continues to take conscious control over what aspects of his notorious history he pays attention to. His choice, clearly, having published more than twenty books since *The Satanic Verses* and the existential melee it provoked, is to focus on feeding his intellectual curiosity and creative appetite.

Eighteen months after the horrifying attempt on his life, Rushdie published a memoir about the ordeal. *Knife: Meditations After an Attempted Murder* is a book he says it was necessary for him to write—"a way to take charge of what happened, and to answer violence with art." Rushdie is exceptional, not just as a writer and thinker but as an example of choosing what to pay attention to; of doing the hard work to take charge of how we are impacted by hardships and uncertainties. If Salman Rushdie can choose to live a creative, outspoken, active public life under the crushing weight of having a bounty on his head—can choose to look, as he told the *New Yorker*, "forwards not backwards," even after an attack that nearly claimed his life—surely the rest of us can choose to be more conscious of our own agency in coping with much less immediate threats.

In the face of what seems like overwhelming change, however unfamiliar and unsettling the patterns of reality around us may appear, we retain influence over our own choices in how to deal with what comes next.

Uncertainty, syn.: *Ambiguity*

"Don't swallow. And no talking until I say so."

I lie prone on an examination table at Women's College Hospital; sweater off, neck slightly arched, studying the tiny perforations in the ceiling tiles above me so as not to catch sight of the large needle being inserted into my throat. The head of the endocrinology department stands over me, passing an ultrasound wand across my thyroid to guide her in the needle biopsy extraction during which I mustn't swallow.

Later, she will show me a surprisingly large vial full of what could pass for strawberry Jell-O but is actually a formaldehyde fluid cocktail of tissue and blood from my thyroid. But right now, I am lying still, not talking, not swallowing.

A recent ultrasound found two oversized nodules on my thyroid, one of which was of some concern. Seventy percent of women have thyroid nodules, the vast majority of which are benign, but this particular one is too big to ignore. There is no connection between breast cancer and thyroid cancer, but melanoma is a cancer cousin (not a medical term, but that's the gist of what the doctor told me) and can sometimes be a side effect of previous radiation treatment.

I had a melanoma removed from my left leg in 2017.

I had radiation on my left side in 2009, as part of my first breast cancer treatment.

Do I even need to tell you which side of my thyroid gland the oversized nodule is on?

The strawberry Jell-O mix will be spun in a lab and analyzed for malignancy; I will have the results within two weeks.

By now this whole routine is unnervingly familiar, like a mathematical equation I've calculated so many times it's committed to memory. (Lump + ultrasound + biopsy) × waiting = breast cancer × (2009 + 2018) (melanoma × 2017).

Which leaves me lying on the examination table staring at the pinprick holes in the ceiling tiles while a pinprick hole is being jabbed in my neck, running some calculus. History of melanoma plus oversized thyroid nodule minus doctor not overly concerned open bracket previous radiation close bracket divided by doctors who couldn't feel my last cancer tumour either multiplied by four months of not feeling well equals ... Well, all it equals is me lying on an examination table having a needle biopsy of a nodule that 70 percent of women have, the results of which will be revealed in about two weeks. Anything beyond that is conjecture, it is worry, it is anxiety-inducing and it is unhelpful. Not interested. Not there yet. Right now it is raining, I'm excited to see my son who returns home from a work trip this evening, and in a few minutes when that needle comes out of my neck I'll be able to put my sweater back on and it is incredibly cozy, one of my favourites. That's not distraction or denial, that's just the way things are at the moment.

GETTING LOST

If I know what I shall find, I do not want to find it.
Uncertainty is the salt of life.
—*Erwin Chargaff,* Heraclitean Fire:
Sketches from a Life Before Nature

WHAT IF SOMETHING THAT feels like an unwelcome change to a plan is actually a better alternative? Possibly even a necessary one. Oftentimes we're under such pressure to execute the intentions we have for a given day, year, or minute, and we've grown so attached to our own assumptions about how that course of action should unfold, that we don't grant ourselves the time or permission to consider all the possibilities. We wind up in an argument with reality, resisting what is happening.

With my ability to move freely put squarely on hold by poor health, and my freedom to expend careless energy no longer something I can take for granted, I've started to wonder how else to think about this besides feeling frustration and despair. I'm trying to look past the limitations my restricted life currently imposes and reframe the uncertainty of tomorrow as an opportunity for discovery. It's a much more hopeful option.

What if this condition of feeling unsettled and anxious over an unpredictable future is in fact a choice? We can choose to think less about what the future holds; we can notice that reflexive impulse telling us we need to know what's coming and catch it before it sets off the dancing monkeys of anxiety. If we choose to be less bound to certainty, other options appear. When we stop being attached to whatever narrative we have assumed will unfold in our lives, what does that look like?

For several glorious years in my early twenties I worked as a bicycle tour guide, leading groups on two-wheeled adventures around Europe. This was in the late 1980s, long before the advent of GPS technology or mobile phones that have made navigation and communication easier. Those were years when setting out on a bicycle in the morning, your possessions packed into a couple of pannier bags hung over your rear wheel, you had nothing but your wits and a folded paper map to get you to your destination. And when the map got wet in the rain, leaving a tattered hole of soggy paper at the crease and a potentially critical gap in the plan of how to get from A to B, you had to get comfortable with figuring it out yourself.

As a guide I translated and navigated and sent everyone on their way each morning with a set of clearly typed route instructions, to be folded and tucked into the front basket of each traveller's bicycle, and a confident "See you at the next hotel in time for cocktails!"

On one memorable afternoon, with a handful of the top-dollar clients riding along with me, I pulled over at the side of the road for a swig of water and realized, with great certainty, that we were well off the planned route and quite possibly very lost. It wasn't long before the others pulled up behind me and realized the same thing.

What happens when we're lost? When the route instructions are gone and the prescribed order of events is abandoned? There is a bit of panic, yes—an instant tallying of all the expensive and possibly life-threatening worst-case scenarios this sudden uncertainty may bring about. But there's also a freedom, an exhilarating free fall as a parallel universe opens up and we slip through a portal into the immediacy of life in all its unknowable randomness.

Getting well and truly lost puts the rest of our fairly prescriptive lives into stark contrast: we see, suddenly, how little freedom there is in routine, how rarely a life made up mostly of planning and executing allows us to brush up against the delicate blossom of raw possibility, to feel the full expanse of what may happen in a given moment.

On that afternoon of cycling, there was muttering among the travellers, some nervous tittering, and more than a little side-eying of the fearless leader who was supposed to know better. But there was something else alongside that too. Somewhere, there was the sound of productive camaraderie and hard work. Voices calling to one another in French, a child's voice laughing, the low rumble of a machine humming along beneath it all.

Roadside in our North American spandex cycling shorts,

we looked around, but all we could see were vineyards on all sides. I turned around and began to pedal off the road and down a narrow gap between the vines. And there, just a few metres away, was a family of vintners harvesting grapes.

The *vendange*! The most important and most glorious time in French wine country. The *vendange*, or harvest, is the celebration of a summer's worth of hard work to grow the grapes to a perfect state of balanced acidic perfection.

I called out to my clients, "Put down your bikes and come over here!"

An old green flatbed truck stood idling in the opening amid the vines. Scattered around it like divers sent out from the mothership were men and women in dusty cotton work clothes, hunched over, making their way along each row of vines. One of the men wandered upright between them, sporting what can only be described as a metal backpack—a deep open-topped bucket into which the others dropped their grapes. They'd lift up their apron-fronts or hoist armfuls of the clippings they'd gathered and toss them in. Eventually, when his pack was full, the man would climb up a small set of steps leaning up against the back of the truck, fold himself over in a jackknife position, and let the grapes spill out over his head. And there, in the bed of the truck, stood the best part of the entire scene: a small boy, no more than six years old, dressed in a white undershirt and denim overalls, stomping gently in his black rubber boots, his slight body just the right size to crush the grapes open.

"Bonjour!" the crew members called out to the ridiculous-looking spandex travellers. "*Bienvenu!*"

I translated for the cyclists as the harvesters welcomed us into their midst and asked if we'd care to help, and handed us each a curious one-handed metal clipper that looked like a bottle opener with a hook. An older man, his friendly face lined with creases that told of many years spent grape-farming in the sun, showed us how to wrap a pinky finger through the loop at one end of the clipper and use the hook at the other end to cut off the clusters of grapes. We followed his directions and drifted, one by one, into this spontaneous adventure that felt more like a reverie, acting out our small roles in a play we'd had no idea we'd ever be cast in. The little boy laughed as he frolicked about in the ever-growing load of grapes in his family's truck; my clients laughed at the utter magic of this day, the late afternoon sun setting slowly on this unlikely scene.

We were lost. We had no idea where we were or who these people were or how to get to our hotel for cocktail hour, but none of that mattered. We had found a moment in life—fresh, real, unforgettable—offered up when we had the good sense to lose our way.

~

Ursula K. Le Guin said the only thing that makes life possible is not knowing what comes next. When we cling to the familiar and the predictable, we surrender the fresh perspective and insights that only come when we navigate unfamiliar territory. In an essay entitled "Making Not Knowing," based on her 2005 commencement address at the School of the

Art Institute of Chicago, American visual artist and professor Ann Hamilton makes the case that we don't arrive by knowing where we're going—that a state of not knowing is essential for creativity. "In every work of art something appears that does not previously exist, and so, by default, you work from what you know to what you don't know."

Most of us have a childhood memory of feeling hot-cheeked shame when called upon by a teacher whose question we were unable to answer. But perhaps "I don't know" is a position we judge too harshly. In times of uncertainty, when our default is to grasp for the security of knowledge, it is easy to reject the liminal state of not knowing. But there are different kinds of not knowing: helpless ignorance is a very different thing to, say, patient curiosity. "Not knowing, waiting and finding … involve work and research," writes Hamilton. "Not knowing is a permissive and rigorous willingness to trust, leaving knowing in suspension, trusting in possibility without result, regarding as possible all manner of response."

It's a state we almost never let ourselves get into, unless we somehow lose our way. The only time we are truly at risk of real danger is when we are checked out, lost and disinterested. Otherwise, being lost actually makes us more mindful—engaged in exploration. When we are lost, we pay attention to details we haven't noticed before; the unfamiliarity of our circumstances demands an override of our selective filtering habit and jolts our eyes and mind open, igniting a spark in the dark recesses of our imagination that are usually bypassed in our habitual patterns of comfort and predictability. What untapped brilliance might lie undiscovered in those recesses? What opportunity lies in the unknown circumstances through which we meander?

From scientific research and development to artistic innovation and creation, not one act of originality has ever emerged from adherence to the familiar, the safe, the predictable. By definition, every creative act births something new. Ingenuity and evolution literally cannot happen without crossing through a liminal state, passing over a threshold into a new way of thinking or seeing or being in the world. Think of the painter who packs up their brushes to paint outdoors, *en plein air*, in order to experience an entirely different relationship with light than they could ever have in a studio. Or the writer who enters a prolific spell of productive creativity while away on a retreat in a new and out-of-routine place. Once, paddling a canoe down a quiet back channel of the Ottawa River, I came upon a barge full of what looked like sound equipment and microphones and a group of musicians wearing headphones and strumming guitars—they had transported their recording studio out onto open water to see what kind of impact the new atmosphere and ambience would have on their songwriting.

Drugs are perhaps the quickest route to a new perspective, the well-worn artist's trope: taking mind-altering substances to find an entryway to a place of creative discovery, to become less attached to the routine. Indigenous peoples took peyote to escape the confines of present certainties and grow closer to the divine; much of ancient Greek sculpture and art celebrates the poppy flower and the creative muse its opium afforded; "Lucy in the Sky with Diamonds," by the day-tripping Beatles, is possibly the most famous artistic tribute to the visionary powers of LSD.

Each has their own avenue to get there, but I think it's safe to say that creators of every kind need to swim about in uncertainty: it's the breeding ground for inspiration, the only place art can ever come from. In a letter to his brothers written in 1817, the Romantic poet John Keats asserted that he'd figured out the key to becoming as great and accomplished a writer as Shakespeare, or what Keats referred to as a "Man of Achievement." The secret was a quality he called negative capability. "That is," he wrote, "when a man is capable of being in uncertainties, mysteries, doubts, without any irritable reaching after fact and reason."

Harvard psychologist Shelley Carson has studied brain imagery in highly creative people to get a scientific understanding of what neurochemistry is at work during acts of invention. Carson's research shows that creative people spend less time using the executive control functions of their brains—things like reason, evaluation, and judgment—and more time in what neuroscientists call the default mode network—absorbing, connecting, and envisioning. The key to achieving those states is something Carson identifies as "cognitive disinhibition," a state in which we are more alert and aware of the unfiltered details around us. A mind that is open to new experiences and ideas is the gateway to so-called *aha!* moments. What seem like flashes of cognitive inspiration are actually formulated below the level of conscious thought. If we don't allow ourselves enough time in those liminal states, uncertain and precarious and open, any potential ideas will fade away before they can surface, shut down by our commanding grip on certainty.

Artists actively seek out the unknown to find what they don't even know they're looking for. Botticelli's *Birth of Venus*, Joni Mitchell's *Clouds*, Van Gogh's *Starry Night*, Bach's Cello Suites, all of Jane Austen—whatever art you love best, every thing of beauty came from individuals who sat in uncertainty and played with it to see what would happen. You can't get the *Mona Lisa* by executing steps in a paint-by-numbers.

The art that appreciates unpredictability most of all must be jazz. Whether or not you appreciate the sounds that happen as a result, jazz musicians execute their craft in a state of happy uncertainty. There is no sure bet about how any performance will unfold—ever. A jazz musician puts their faith in just a couple of simple things: their own well-trained physical dexterity, and the fundamental rhythm of the tune.

Some of the most sophisticated compositions by Duke Ellington—among the most iconic jazz musicians and masters of the form—were inspired by things that happened in the moment on stage. Dexter Gordon, the iconic American tenor saxophonist, believed every stage performance is a communication with the audience; since every audience is different, so were the notes he played in his solos from night to night. Dizzy Gillespie's performance of bebop jazz was affectionately known as "the sound of surprise," full of speedy chord changes that no one saw coming.

Herbie Hancock tells a story of performing in Stuttgart, Germany, as the piano player on tour with Miles Davis. He was playing "So What," one of Davis's compositions from the 1950s, with Wayne Shorter on sax, Ron Carter on bass, and Tony Williams playing drums. Right in the middle of Davis's solo, "I played the wrong chord," recalls Hancock. "A chord that sounded completely wrong, like a big mistake." It was such a mistake, in fact, that he gasped out loud and put his hands up to his ears. But the best part of the story is what happened next: "Miles paused for a second, and then he played some notes that made my chord *right*. Miles was able to make something that was wrong into something that was right, with the choice of the notes that he played."

There's a reason Miles Davis is revered as one of the ultimate jazz legends, and this is one small example of his genius. But it's an example of something else as well: if that live jazz concert performance is a metaphor for the sometimes-dizzying chaos of life, the ability to continue steadily along even when the unexpected happens lies in the attitude we bring to those unplanned events that at first blush might appear to be a disaster. It's about keeping cool.

"What I realize now is that Miles didn't hear it as a mistake," Hancock says. "He heard it as something that happened. Just an event. And so that was part of the reality of what was happening at that moment. And he dealt with it. Since he didn't hear it as a mistake, he was able to find something to do with it." That's negative capability right there.

Hancock, a legendary improvisational artist in his own right, still draws on the memory of what he learned from Davis playing live in that high-stakes performance in Stuttgart. "We can look for the world to be as we would like it to be as individuals. But the important thing is that we grow. The only way we grow is to have a mind that is open enough to experience situations as they are and to turn poison into medicine. Take whatever situation you have and make something constructive happen with it."

That's what we give up if we cleave too closely to the familiar. As frightening and destabilizing as it often feels, uncertainty is the only real space where new information can come into view. Randomness. Epiphanies. Fresh ideas. Innovative approaches. They can result in some of our favourite experiences when they happen—but they only happen outside of certainty. The best meals you eat in a city or neighbourhood you're visiting are often the ones you discover after getting disoriented and turned around from where you'd planned to go, so you ask a local and stumble upon a treasure. In that uncertainty, you are receptive to the possibility of something good.

But you don't have to wait until you wind up hopelessly lost in a new place to experience that opening up of possibility. Curiosity is an option every day, even in the most familiar of circumstances. By definition, being curious leaves us open to exploration, to meandering, to seeing what happens. Just as every artist relies on curiosity to lead them forward through the unknown, and every scientific breakthrough is preceded by a hunger for knowledge, we all can cultivate curiosity as a habit. Bring it along on those awe walks, and it will hugely amplify your capacity to experience wonder. It takes the mind off the paved highway of cognitive bias and shifts past all we think we know, illuminating new pathways that lead to new ideas and perspectives. Curiosity is a superpower, a critical tool for approaching challenges of every kind. Without it, we find ourselves back in the certainty trap.

In my quest for different ways to frame the idea of uncertainty, I've been reading Rick Rubin's *The Creative Act: A Way of Being*. I was curious about the mysteries of the creative process—essentially a state of not knowing—as observed by the man who has been called the most important music producer of his time. Rubin is a legend, and if you don't know his name, you've definitely heard his work: he has produced hit records with Run DMC, Public Enemy, the Strokes, the Red Hot Chili Peppers, the Chicks, Johnny Cash, and many more; he co-founded Def Jam records, and helped bring the hip-hop genre to the mainstream. How do you become that kind of hitmaker? Rubin doesn't have much in the way of technical producing or performing skills—he barely plays any instruments, and he can't work a soundboard. His talent, by all accounts—including his own—lies in his ability to listen, to be open to possibilities, and to ask the right questions that lead the artists to find their way to the best music they can make.

Rubin's approach to his work is a powerful example of not being attached to outcomes. To the extent he has any plan at all when he walks into a recording studio, it is to create a state of uncertainty from which new possibilities may flow; relying on what Albert Einstein called the "sacred gift" of the intuitive mind. Rubin has experienced, in his decades of breaking ground in the music business—and hitting platinum along the way—that there is great power in not knowing. It frees us up to progress, untethered as we are to assumptions. "Curiously," he writes, "not being aware of a challenge may be just what we need to rise to it."

John Cleese takes the value of not knowing even further. In a 1991 lecture about creativity, the beloved comedy giant argued that we cannot ever reach the point of creative innovation without first inhabiting a state of playfulness—in which we trust that we don't know what will happen, and that whatever happens is okay. Essentially, this is the defining principle of improv comedy. "You cannot be playful if you're frightened that moving in some direction will be wrong, something you shouldn't have done … You've got to risk saying things that are silly and illogical and wrong. And the best way to get the confidence to do that is to know that while you're being creative, nothing is wrong."

But why is it so hard for adults to take those risks, to feel comfortable in the uncertainty of free-form playfulness, to allow ourselves to believe that nothing we say or do is "wrong"?

If I were to drive today past the small, red-brick home of my early childhood, the tree in the southeast corner of the little backyard would likely resemble any other old pine—if it is still there at all. But as a young girl, that far corner (not far at all really, in adult steps) held immense possibility. Crawling beneath the low branches of the big Jack pine allowed entry to a secret world—a tunnel only I could fit through that led to a landscape uncharted by my mother, unknown to my father. The floor was a soft cushion of fallen pine needles; the drooping branches above blocked out any reminder of the familiar sights and real-world cues of the yard beyond. *Where does this network of branch tunnels lead to? What else is here? Where am I right now?* Those musings were what drew me back to that corner, deep into a space that felt unknown, where I was risking my safety.

Driving past today, you would see that in fact the neighbour's garden was but a few feet away—no parallel universe ever existed under that tree, no danger lay waiting for my young wandering self. But then, smaller of limb and larger of imagination and trust, I felt a deep love for the unpredictability of what might be possible under there. At the end of an afternoon's play, emerging onto the plain grass of our little lawn, my baby brother's cries ringing out of the window of the house, I would experience the feeling anyone once lost will recall: a distinct mix of relief at recognizing where you are and disappointment that the heightened aliveness of being lost and missing, if only in your own mind, is over.

There's a disorientation to being adrift in the unfamiliar; the trick lies in how we feel about that bewilderment. As Daniel Boone, the Euro-American trespasser nicknamed the "Columbus of the woods," reportedly said of his lengthy sojourns in the wilderness: "I never got lost, but I will admit to being bewildered for three days." He never doubted he'd find his way. Perhaps that is the secret for the rest of us non-colonial conquerors too: the confidence to embrace being lost, knowing that we can handle it.

As much as I have thanked Google Maps for shortening a route through urban traffic or handily clarifying travel time on a road trip, a part of me curses it too. Our reliance on technology is an automatic surrendering of our wits: our internal compass grows weak and impotent when we never challenge it to help us find our way.

I miss getting lost. I miss the lightheaded heart-stop of that realization when nothing is recognizable, nothing makes sense, and no one knows where I am, including me. There is a bliss that opens up, albeit twinned with worry. It's like slipping briefly into a parallel universe in which you are Alice, in a Wonderland that holds endless possibilities. When was the last time you were really stumped as to your whereabouts, which route to take, the direction of home?

Getting lost on a bicycle on the charming side roads of a foreign country was more than just an occasion to pause, evaluate the situation, pull out a local language phrasebook and hone my orientation skills. It was an open door to an entirely different state of being: surrendering the plan, paying closer attention to whatever was right in front of me, feeling things more deeply. Gathered with fellow travellers at the day's end, sharing tales of our adventures over dinner, the best stories—exuberantly told with sparkly eyed delight—were inevitably from those who had somehow wandered offtrack. Who became most alive when they found themselves lost.

A friend of a friend is an occupational therapist who specializes in helping children with emotional dysregulation calm their nervous systems, to be better able to concentrate and cooperate in school. She suggested I might be able to settle and manage some of my various physical symptoms—the buzzing legs, the racing heart, the ringing in my ears, the fluttering nausea—by stimulating my vagus nerve. *Google it*, she said. *You'll find lots of strategies and therapies to activate the vagus nerve.* The idea is to release stress and activate the parasympathetic nervous system, which sends the body into rest and relaxation mode.

After a brief misstep looking through therapist listings in Las Vegas—her advice having been given over the phone—I found the correct spelling and, as promised, a host of vagus therapy techniques. The vagus, I learned, is the longest cranial nerve. Pneumogastric, it relates to both the respiratory and the digestive systems. In fact, the vagus nerve reaches into most of the body: throat, lungs, heart, stomach, liver, spleen, pancreas, kidney, and gut, both large and small intestines. Its name derives from the Latin for "wandering." Though its etymology surely comes from its physical shape and meandering web-like neural network, I can't help but see a message in there: to relax and heal, my body literally needs to wander more. Wandering is like walking with uncertainty. Wandering into wonder.

I tap above my belly button. I tug gently on my earlobes. I touch the back of my neck and cast my eyes to the left and the right, breathing deeply. Each vagus therapy exercise looks and sounds more whimsical and absurd than the next, but there is no mistaking the immediate wave of calm that washes over me as I follow these quirky steps. I have no idea what I'm doing, but it works. Lost in the not knowing, I yawn, sigh, and observe a gentle reprieve in my physical discomfort. I have wandered off the path and don't know how to get back. But look at all that there is to be found here.

It seems to me that the safety and comfort we seek, that we mistakenly believe will be found in the arms of the familiar and predictable, is right there and present in the uncertain. We just have to learn to recognize all the value the liminal holds.

Uncertainty, syn.: *Inconclusiveness*

At my rheumatology appointment, I start to cry. What am I even doing in the hospital's rheumatology department? I barely understand what rheumatology is. The study of diseases that affect the joints, muscles, and blood vessels—things like lupus, rheumatoid arthritis, and various conditions I've never heard of. I had to google it.

The doctor is reed-thin, his length and height somehow accentuated by his pointy narrow shoes. His poofy mushroom-cap hairdo belongs in a 1980s music video, but otherwise he is all business. Kindly but robotic. No greeting as he ushers me into his office. No facial expression as he responds to my too-long tale, the one I'm now so sick of recounting: tingly head and deep sinus headache that started almost exactly six months ago; headaches, nausea, fatigue, tinnitus, aching feet. Even I get lost on the circuitous trail of my symptoms. When I describe the fiery bubbles running through my veins, he stares straight into his computer screen, stumped for what to type. Buzzy skin is not a symptom he knows what to do with.

He palpates the joints of my hand, touches his long cool fingers to my temples. *Does this hurt?* It doesn't. *Do you have pain in your tongue?* That's a new one; but no, I don't.

It's when he asks me what I do for a living that the emotion swells. I describe what I *did*, what I now describe as my "old life": hosting live radio ... fast-paced ... sharp wit ... quick responses to the unfolding news of the day ... It feels so far away now, the ability to move quickly, the determination to ask hard questions and carry out important conversations, the energy to laugh and crack jokes. I barely remember that version of myself. I miss her. Did I cherish the days when energy and vigour felt like cheap and bottomless commodities? Will I ever be able to take that spirited full life for granted again? Will I ever be able to work again?

The lanky rheumatologist does not look like the type who'd offer a shoulder to cry on as I unburden myself of my cumulative worries, so I reel back the sorrow. Within a gentle inhale I restore the calm, positive, friendly patient that is my standard presentation at medical appointments. Doctors are busy people, the system is overwhelmed; my bizarre and seemingly endless health mystery is something they cannot be expected to take on emotionally or in any great depth.

Without a word, the doctor stands up and walks out of his office. Did he notice some emotion come over me and want to give me a minute? A moment later he returns and sits back down at his computer without any explanation.

After typing for another minute, he turns and says he has no idea what's the matter with me but he is certain that I do not have a rheumatological condition. I think that is probably a good thing, but at this point I can hardly tell. I am so adrift in this wide-open ocean of undiagnosed medical uncertainty, I am almost disappointed to be told I do not have scleroderma or spondyloarthritis. I realize I should not joke about how serious those conditions are, but that's just it: I'm not joking. There is a part of me that would trade the endless months of traipsing along the path of uncertainty for the hard, grim dead-end of a terrible diagnosis. I can't possibly mean that, and yet there are times when I truly do.

STATES OF PANIC

For, you see, so many out-of-the-way things had happened lately, that Alice had begun to think that very few things indeed were really impossible.
—*Lewis Carroll,* Alice's Adventures in Wonderland

UNPRECEDENTED. THAT WORD WAS used and overused during much of 2020, for good reason. The unfolding of the global pandemic was a string of events equal parts unfamiliar, terrifying, and destabilizing. There isn't really one flashbulb moment for the turning point, no singular *where were you when . . . ?* The blows of uncertainty came in a battering progression, the Jenga blocks plucked out in rapid succession from the tenuous tower of our collective well-being and semblance of certitude.

The World Health Organization declaring a global pandemic. Tom Hanks announcing he had the virus, somehow the tangible proof this terror was real. Overrun emergency rooms. Ventilator shortages. Grandparents dying alone in locked-down care facilities. Two of my three boys, in quarantine after returning home from abroad, sequestered in a neighbour's basement apartment; dropping food at their door and waving at our babies through glass. Standing in the middle of my kitchen—sheltering in place, such a cozy euphemism for the abject isolation and entrapment of lockdown—my head a mad arcade of unanswerable questions. *How much longer will this go on? What will happen to my parents? What if the food supplies run out? Who do we know who will die?* Only the March weather remained unimpacted by the global crisis; its bleak damp chill dragged relentlessly on.

If we imagine our ability to feel some certainty about life and generally familiar with our world sits on a shelf, it's like 2020 hired a reckless, unlicensed carpenter, who showed up and started repositioning the shelf higher and higher up the wall. Each of us is equipped with a different degree of coping skills, which would be height and perhaps arm length in this analogy. Some of us were unable to reach the shelf sooner than others. But eventually it was too high for us all. What in the actual fuck was happening, and whatever could we do about it? Anxiety came on like an avalanche.

Whatever your experience of COVID-19's tumultuous arrival, existential fear and overwhelming uncertainty were a huge part of it. Adrift, held in a limbo of foreboding, each of us was thrust into a state of unknowing as a genie of angst-ridden confusion burst out of the bottle. That narrative of terror and tragedy is one painful and sobering truth of the pandemic. But it is by no means the only narrative. Had we, back in mid-2020, rushed to judge that all was lost, had we only paid attention in the ensuing months and years to the trauma-filled headlines and the doomsayers, there is a lot we would have missed. In the spirit of choosing what we pay attention to, let's widen the lens.

For many people, the existential bewilderment of the pandemic was a call to a more conscious way of living. The painful uncertainty and struggle brought on by a novel virus and global lockdowns became a humbling reminder of our collective vulnerability and a trigger to live this "one wild and precious life," to quote poet Mary Oliver, with greater intention. That's the flip side of uncertainty—if everything can be taken away from us, it must therefore be treasured.

The Great Reinvention, as it has been called, saw people in every sector decide to shake things up—to seek out change. The uncertainty and unpredictability of the pandemic years became for many a motivator to live a more meaningful life. *If not now, then when* was the driver for imagining a different way of being—for pursuing long-shelved dreams and interests.

People took up hobbies during lockdown, discovering passions they had perhaps been putting off. Baking, learning a language, playing an instrument, gardening. People found solace in leaning into the isolation, and discovered flow, purpose, and presence in the very close and small. Depression, anxiety, and other mental health challenges ballooned during the pandemic years, but so did society's willingness to talk about those struggles openly and call for more support. What also increased during the peak of the pandemic was altruism. The *World Happiness Report* showed that volunteering, donating to charity, and helping strangers were all happening more frequently in 2021 than in previous years. Instinctively during that global crisis, many people figured out the pattern for how to manage uncertainty: taking small and meaningful actions to control what we can helps to ease our suffering.

In the mid-1990s, American psychologist Richard Tedeschi coined the term *post-traumatic growth* to describe what he saw in his research as a positive outcome that many people experience after going through something exquisitely harrowing and traumatic. "People develop new understandings of themselves, the world they live in, how to relate to other people, the kind of future they might have and a better understanding of how to live life."

Of course, when crisis strikes, we're not usually thinking about all the growth and character-building it will afford us once we get through it. But if we could bear that in mind, it might temper the reflexive urge to panic. There's a chain reaction that happens to produce panic, a systematic acceleration from small concern to giant blown-up fear—the cycle of anxiety. It's a recognizable pattern, and it happens to us all; the trick is to be able to interrupt the cycle. The cognitive behavioural approach to anxiety is to recognize the thoughts that are causing all those frantic feelings and bring some rational understanding to why they're happening (and then explore alternatives to the unhelpful thoughts).

Our rush to panic is rooted in two things: fear that we cannot handle whatever strange new problem has beset us, and the vaguely arrogant notion that we shouldn't have to. Our primal wiring to seek out safety and security tricks us into believing that there is an ideal, everything-is-under-control version of life in which we no longer need to deal with hardships. I hope, by this point in the book—if not in life more broadly—you can see the folly in that fantasy. (And the trouble it causes us.)

A far more helpful approach, and one I'm learning to embrace in my ongoing stretch of poor health, is to think of life as a series of challenges to be dealt with. They're never not coming for us, so why not accept that and meet them head on. Think of top tennis players, poised and eager at the baseline. They don't panic when a ball comes at them from an unusual angle. Problems, changes of plan, dashed expectations, losses, hardships—life is bound to serve these challenges into our court. So loosen up, grip your racquet, and stand ready. There's really no other way.

We are all competitors in life's grand obstacle course, navigating hurdles of varying duration and scale. Try to imagine what meaning or purpose life would have *without* obstacles. Yes, it would be dreamy for a while—that's called a vacation—but without any challenges to meet, what would we ... do? How would we grow? When we think like that, each new threat—even the most existential-seeming—appears in a softer light.

Consider the trajectory of your emotional response to artificial intelligence in the past couple of years. On the list of forces that are currently destabilizing our sense of certainty, AI surely ranks close to the top. With wildly disruptive powers and great potential for social harm, it has brought about a low-grade panic. AI can hack passwords;

it can ace law school admission tests; ChatGPT can write a high school essay in less time than it takes to boil water. When images of Pope Francis wearing Balenciaga went viral, many of the millions sharing the unlikely image never thought to question its credibility. Was the supreme pontiff really tricked out in streetwear and cruising the Vatican with hip-hop swagger? What other manipulated images could we be (or have we already been) fooled into believing are real? Artificially generated figures like humans with horse heads or Mahatma Gandhi taking a selfie can be disorienting, an experiential daze, and there is a proliferation of software that puts that power in anyone's hands. What might those hands do with it? We laugh at the videos in which AI replicates the voices of past presidents and creates a mock dust-up between Obama, Biden, and Trump; we laugh less when a doting senior is scammed out of her savings by the artificially replicated voice of her grandchild calling for help.

There are also geopolitical complications arising from the misuse of AI. Among the most dire are what's known as deepfakes: hyper-realistic digital forgeries in which moving images are manipulated in ways that make them indistinguishable from reality. These manipulations are so advanced that governments must fear the consequences of a world leader doing or saying something they in fact never did or said. (Think of the video that surfaced on social media roughly a month after Russia invaded Ukraine, in which Ukraine's president Volodymyr Zelensky appeared to tell his troops to surrender.) In 2018, waaaay back in the early days of AI, the US Congress sent a letter to the director of national intelligence outlining their grave concerns about the unrestrained development of deepfakes. "By blurring the line between fact and fiction, deepfake technology could undermine public trust in recorded images and video as objective depictions of reality." There are forecasts predicting that, by 2026, 90 percent of online content may be synthetically generated. Several titles on a "must-read summer 2025 books" list published in a number of respected newspapers do not in fact exist, the list—and most of the books it recommended—having been generated by AI and never fact-checked by a human. Add to the equation the fact that AI is currently being trained with synthetic data *created by AI*, every generation of AI model less accurate than the one before it, and the notion of accuracy drifts even farther out of reach. An information apocalypse, some fear, is dawning.

Artificial intelligence is a real and present threat to many of the systems that have long sustained the functioning of human society. AI is a significant enough disruptive societal force that it has its own section in the *New York Times* and its own ministry in Canada's federal government, attempts at rigorously monitoring and interpreting the rapidly evolving technology that has radically uprooted our collective understanding of what is real and of how the world works.

If you have been losing sleep over the potential harm that artificial intelligence may cause in our world, you're in good company. Sundar Pichai, chief executive at Google, has admitted to lying awake at night himself, worrying about the great harm that may come if such technology is deployed wrongly. Pichai is one of many who has called for a global regulatory framework for AI, akin to the treaties that regulate nuclear arms use. (Why is it, by the way, that the people who are the most anxious about the doomsday potential of technology and its societal impacts are the very tech wizards who created the technology in the first place? Only after having profited handsomely from developing algorithms and artificial intelligence to keep kids hooked on their phone or make YouTube videos more addictive or personalize advertisements on social media and create echo chambers in our digital lives, do successful tech giants stop to assess the impact of their work with some degree of alarm and remorse.)

At a 2017 conference on artificial intelligence, a set of governance principles was established for AI development, acknowledging that "advanced AI could represent a profound change in the history of life on Earth, and should be planned for and managed with commensurate care and resources." Unfortunately, that care and planning has taken a back seat in the race to expand AI's capacity. Developers are so focused on what is technically possible, they're not thinking about the consequences and what kind of world their handiwork may bring about.

Consternation over the impact of the artificial intelligence revolution is so heightened it has its own moniker: *AInxiety*. Though it's probably worth noting, as we barrel down the luge track of hysteria, that nearly every advancement in technology has brought about widespread hand-wringing. Worries such as computerphobia, computer anxiety, and technostress emerged as early as the 1980s. "Despite the growing role of computers in society, some individuals may actually avoid and resist learning about computers due to their anxiety," began a 1987 research paper entitled "Assessing Computer Anxiety: Development and Validation of the Computer Anxiety Rating Scale." There is, of course, ample evidence to show the deleterious effects of too much screentime and the disconnect from the natural world in favour of a digital device. But it would be wildly inaccurate to characterize *everything* about the advent of personal computers, smartphones, the internet, and any other technological advances as entirely problematic or world-ending. It's also worth noting that AI is impressive and in-demand based on its lightning-speed access to and regurgitation of other things—things that already existed. From where I sit, that makes AI fast and mighty, but not creative or original.

The Gartner Hype Cycle, developed by American IT firm Gartner, a consultancy group specializing in technology insights for business, is a framework that tracks the stages of response to new technologies. People typically go through periods of excitement, disillusionment, and then acceptance when faced with a huge technological change—a pattern you may recognize in your own feelings about AI.

We know about its potential for misuse and human job loss, but what *else* is true about artificial intelligence? If we quell the AInxiety for a moment and shift our attention elsewhere, what do we find? We might see ourselves asking Siri to text a friend while we're driving, or getting surprisingly thorough answers to a Google search query from the search engine's AI overview. We may notice how easily we can access translations of text or audio in any language, or how much more detail AI can observe on X-rays or MRIs than the human eye. Hospitals across North America now use AI software to detect incremental changes in bone density that are early indications of the risk of osteoporosis. AI is improving efficiencies in almost every medical testing department, speeding up scans and thereby reducing the time patients are waiting for answers. And the human technicians, who may have once feared that artificial intelligence would eclipse the need for their own, are now finding that their skills are complementary, and that the faster pace of testing requires even more human staff to support.

Hollywood's use of AI to de-age actors is at once an unsettling novelty for audiences, a potential threat to young actors who will no longer be cast to play the junior versions of famous stars, and another tool in the filmmaker's storytelling kit. In the rush to panic, the initial assumption can be that it's all bad, but much of the media's response to the introduction of AI techniques is more histrionic than accurate.

"The Beatles Are Back!" screamed many a headline, typical of the overblown response to Sir Paul McCartney's announcement in 2023 that a previously unreleased Beatles song had been brought to life from an old demo of a John Lennon composition, found on a cassette labelled "For Paul" after his death. "We were able to take John's voice and get it pure through this AI," McCartney told the BBC. The application of AI allowed for the "cleaning up" of this at-home recording to extract Lennon's vocals in a way that had never been possible before. It also allowed McCartney to include some "duets" with Lennon on a recent tour. Does that amount to a diabolical tinkering with reality? Some musical purists think so; others just appreciate being able to hear the famous vocal partnership that changed music history made possible once again through artificial intelligence. And isn't the synthesizer itself a version of AI fakery? Mimicking a range of instrumentation with the push of a button? But how do we take advantage of the beneficial applications of AI without losing our way amid its potential for harm?

For Rick Rubin, it was an ancient game that influenced his response to the advent of computers that think for themselves. Go is a strategy contest that is considered the oldest board game in the world, invented in China nearly three thousand years ago. AlphaGo is an AI program specifically built to play Go—and in *The Creative Act,* Rubin describes a five-game match played between the program and a human grandmaster. At a critical juncture, it was the computer's turn to make a move. There were—by all assumptions on the part of the grandmaster and every other student of the game who was watching—only two choices the computer could possibly make. So when AlphaGo made a third, utterly unforeseen choice, the crowd was shocked; meanwhile, the grandmaster was so indignant he had to get up and leave the table for several minutes to regain his composure. When he did return and played out the game, another unthinkable happened: the computer won. In the end, the computer won four out of the five games.

A lot of people would interpret this outcome as portentous—a sign of the inevitable robot overthrow of all human endeavour. For Rubin, there is an entirely different way to look at it. On an episode of the podcast *Broken Record* with author and interviewer Malcolm Gladwell, Rubin pointed out that the computer won not by knowing more, but by knowing less. Free of the thousands of years' worth of cultural norms and expectations about how to play the game, the computer system was not limited by a sense of how it was *supposed* to do things. It was able to approach the game board with a fresh perspective, and thus was able to introduce a new—and victorious—strategy.

How hard it is for us humans to let go of a rush to judgment, and look past the way we think things are supposed to go. How counterintuitive it feels to stop struggling against what is happening, and let go of our resistance to what is right in front of us. How challenging it is to open ourselves up to the possibilities inherent in every change.

I think it's the rate at which this technology is evolving that rattles us most. AI is changing almost at the speed of light—a clip that far outpaces our ability to understand it and interpret how it will impact our ways of living. Which leaves AI as a vast, shapeshifting unknown. It is true that it will continue to bring about changes that we will need to adjust to. It is also true that the technology will be used to spread misinformation and cause an erosion of trust in what we see and hear online. Lawmakers are moving at a sluggish pace compared to AI itself, but regulations are still coming together.

In the meantime, take a closer look at whatever pain or stress you feel about the uncertainty around AI. Our inability to wrap our minds around exactly what impact this technology will have on our individual and collective outcomes is upsetting because of our desire to know—or control—what is happening. Of course, we cannot possibly know what will happen, so can we instead allow our discomfort to point us toward action rather than fear? If AI threatens to make us all more disconnected and distrustful of one another, what kind of conscious action can we take to find meaning and connection as a countermeasure?

I focus on things I know I can trust. I can lean into my own real intelligence, researching and staying informed, and educate myself about the risks and misapplications of AI. For me, there is a fundamental bogusness that underlies the technology. The discomfort stirred up by AI is rooted in my unease toward anything artificial, and so seeking authenticity and genuine connectedness feels like an antidote to that discomfort—and something that is within my sphere of influence. The more time I spend in nature, or in person with people I love, the less troubled I am by unnatural substitutes.

The artificial intelligence revolution is without doubt a generation-defining change. But the idea that it will inevitably ruin all we hold dear seems patently inaccurate, and not a basis for panic. Developing trust in the way forward sometimes starts with looking back; after all, we have survived unprecedented social change before. Your heart has been broken before, we have survived great loss before, I have emerged back to full health before. It's helpful to call on that history as fuel for the way forward. As Helen Keller wrote in her book *Optimism*, "Although the world is full of suffering, it is also full of the overcoming of it."

I once heard someone describe life as a pointillist painting. When we get too hung up on our own point of view and on the details of our own small experience of the world, it's like we look too closely at those tiny dots and thus fail to see the whole picture. When we transcend our own individual selves by staying curious, being open to awe and wonder, and connecting with others, it pulls back our perspective, allowing for a more complete view of the canvas. And in the process, life's uncertainty becomes easier to bear.

Uncertainty, syn: *Puzzle*

Could this be long COVID?

I have asked that question a lot, both of myself and my GP, but my doctor doesn't know a lot about long COVID. Infectious disease specialists don't know a lot about long COVID at this point, so how could an overwhelmed family doctor in a busy downtown practice in a city where 40 percent of people cannot access a primary care physician on the heels of a global pandemic that is nowhere near over in spite of everyone wanting it to be and everyone wanting doctors to have all the answers—

But I mean, really, aren't I a match for almost all the symptoms? Google thinks so.

Fatigue, check.

Muscle weakness and achiness, check.

Bouts of nausea, tinnitus, inability to exercise, sleep disturbances, low blood oxygen, heart palpitations, checkity check check check.

But long COVID is a diagnosis of exclusion. Which means there is no blood test, no easy way to confirm it but to rule out every other possible scenario. It's the side-of-the-freeway motel you finally book into at the end of an exhausting road trip, having driven up and back down every possible off-ramp to check out all the bigger and more reputable hotels, but none has any vacancies so you have to get back on the highway and keep going until you end up at the place with the bulbs burnt out on the sign, but the proprietor, unshaven and reeking of exhaustion and sweat, says: *Sure, c'mon in, there's a room for you down the hall. Door's unlocked.*

A CLIMATE OF CRISIS

> Inaction breeds doubt and fear. Action breeds confidence and courage. If you want to conquer fear, do not sit home and think about it.
>
> —*Dale Carnegie*

I HAVE COME TO a cottage on the shores of the Ottawa River for a week of writing and rest. My host is a dear and lifelong friend, three decades my senior and recently widowed, whose daily afternoon rest time and early-to-bed schedule suit my limited energy. Eight months into this dark tunnel of chronic weariness and discomfort, being here on a peaceful island, surrounded by summer birdsong and the gentle sway of forest branches, is the respite I need. No distractions, no responsibilities beyond self-care; the rest of the world feels far away.

I've set up a little writing spot on the screened veranda, looking southward at the islands scattered down the river, the occasional tin fishing boat passing through the foreground at a slow putt. Today I sit bundled in blankets and the few warm layers I brought along, the forecasted sun for this week nowhere in sight. But something else is off this morning besides the chill; things feel oppressive, socked in. The river is calm, but the scale feels disorienting—more like looking across a wide ocean or into a pale abyss. The distant islands have all but disappeared from view. I know they're there, but I can't see them through the pervasive cloud of light grey.

What is *all that grey?* It's too late in the day for morning mist to still be lifting, and too dry for fog. Unsettled, I check the weather app on my phone. A bright red map appears, a pinpoint of my location pulsing at its centre like a desperate heartbeat. *The health risk for your current location is high*, reads a weather advisory concerning air quality. *Consider reducing or rescheduling strenuous activities outdoors if you experience symptoms such as coughing and throat irritation.* I suddenly recall waking up a few times in the night with a dry cough and wondering if this was one of my symptoms flaring up—but no, here we are on the border of Quebec, one of the many Canadian provinces that is ablaze this summer with wildfires. This dry, thick haze is actually smoke. *The primary pollutant is called PM2.5, particles that are small enough to enter the bloodstream, typically resulting from wildfires, smokestacks, or bacteria.*

Wildfire smoke is a mixture of hazardous air pollutants, including hydrocarbons and lead. As well as contaminating the air with these toxic pollutants, wildfires release large quantities of carbon dioxide and other greenhouse gases into the atmosphere, further impacting the climate. Wildfires are a seasonal norm in many parts of Canada, standard-issue summer disasters that cause more disruption and devastation with every passing year. But the asperity of 2023's season is already record-setting. Every part of the country is literally on fire, the impact of which will be felt for many more months, as far away as Florida. Before this epic ruination is over, nearly fifty million acres of land will be destroyed, and thousands and thousands of people displaced.

Wildfires are how this part of the world is experiencing the reality of climate change at the moment, but the crisis is omnipresent. The earth has warmed—irreparably—since preindustrial times, and that pattern looks set to continue. A European Union climate modelling agency showed record-breaking temperatures month after month in 2023; data from the US National Centers for Environmental Information, part of the National Oceanic and Atmospheric Administration, shows that the past nine years have been the nine warmest on record. We know that trajectory will continue for as long as the burning of fossil fuels continues, which it is predicted to do; human consumption and pollution only continue to escalate, in spite of the urgency. Polar ice caps melt and recede, oceans warm, species decline, and the quality of air and water—the essentials for human life—deteriorate before our eyes. Apocalyptic temperature spikes, droughts, ice storms, and floods kill millions of people every year. The climate crisis is the most existential—and ubiquitous—of all uncertainties.

And yet we continue on our merry, expansion-economy way, desperately attached to a permanent growth model that is clearly no longer feasible. Humans are wired to believe in our own right to be here, and in the relative stability of our future. We go to sleep at night with near-total faith that the sun will rise for us again tomorrow—just as it did today—and that the earth will keep on keeping on. That faith underpins humanity's continued insistence on burning oil, spewing carbon, eliminating species, and polluting and poisoning the water sources that sustain us. No matter how many climate-related disasters we witness, we persist in our habitual, consumptive patterns.

Science journalist David Suzuki once remarked on the overwhelming number of parents who carry an asthmatic child into the hospital emergency room with a breathing impairment, while leaving their gas-guzzling SUV in the parking lot. Some kind of neurological glitch or override seems to create a basic disconnect between our actions and their consequences. British psychoanalyst Sally Weintrobe, a member of the Climate Psychology Alliance, attributes our apparent refusal to change our ruinous ways—even in the face of mounting evidence that we must—to a kind of anxiety. In her book *Engaging with Climate Change: Psychoanalytic and Interdisciplinary Perspectives*, she describes a complex human defence strategy in which we see reality but also don't see reality at the same time, based on what she characterizes as our narcissistic sense of entitlement—believing in our right to be immune to emotional difficulties. That behaviour has earned our species its own title in the geological timeline of the planet: this is the Anthropocene, an era defined by human's presence on Earth. Humankind as a geological force—a dubious honour. Our planet is fucked.

I look out across this wide majestic stretch of the Ottawa River, uncharacteristically pale, and register the gravity of the eerie scene. A helicopter sputters overhead, its looming presence adding to the apprehension. I call out to my friend to come inside, worried for her octogenarian lungs as she gardens in the outdoor air she escaped the city to enjoy. I notice the impulse to fix this, to do something, to push away this unnatural occurrence—to make this terrible, frightening, messed-up thing go away. But short of limiting outdoor activity and possibly wearing a mask, it doesn't feel like there is anything I *can* do. Still, I struggle to surrender to something so wrong, so outside the natural order.

The marching band of climate anxiety—the one that thrums constantly on low volume every waking hour of these unpredictable days—is ramping up to a blaring cacophony of discord. Permafrost melting in Siberia, landslides in Cameroon, flash floods and monsoons in India, historic flooding in Rwanda, unprecedented droughts in California and Mexico, a record number of billion-dollar disasters in the United States this year alone. What kind of human suffering am I contributing to every time I drive a car? How many millions of people will be displaced because of extreme weather, and where will they find safety? What kind of political instability will ensue, as the evolving climate upsets the global hierarchy? I gather my blankets more tightly around me and shuffle off the porch in a jittery stew.

My host and I spend the next three days of our June holiday, perforce, indoors with the doors and windows closed. One day we mask up and venture out for food at the local farmers' market, where the produce is noticeably puny for this time of year. The vendors are apologetic for their smaller crops and limited offerings. "The wildfire smoke is literally blocking out the sun our plants need to grow," one anguished farmer tells us. She throws her hands up and shakes her head, speechless with despair. Her silence speaks volumes. This is our climate-changed, unsafe, hazardous world. This is the life we lead now. And the truth is that no matter how broken the earth's systems feel today, they are in better shape than they will be tomorrow. Next summer's wildfires will most likely be worse.

How do we sit in such deeply unsettling discomfort? The very air we have no choice but to breathe is unfit for human health. How to quell the rising anxiety about this terrifying life? There is no wishing this away; getting back to the plan of a robust planet is well outside any one individual's power. I ache with the oppressive weight of climate uncertainty and my powerlessness in the face of it.

There is no solution at hand for this experience. There is investment in alternative energy sources and the carbon tax on polluters and the preservation of green spaces and the protection of species at risk, and myriad other conservation strategies to mitigate the impending global peril. But right now it all feels like so much *blah blah blah*, as Greta Thunberg would say. Now, here, in this smoky discomfort, there is just the immediate fear and unease of a crisis. That human impulse to be immune to emotional difficulty roils, thwarted and uncomfortable.

The World Health Organization calls climate change the

biggest threat facing humanity. Whipping oneself into a frenzy of consternation over that overarching terror is easy, and the evidence shows that's what is happening. Britt Wray is a leading researcher at the intersection of mental health and climate change, the director of CIRCLE, a climate resilience project at Stanford School of Medicine, and the author of *Generation Dread: Finding Purpose in an Age of Climate Change*. According to her research, 45 percent of young people around the world report that thoughts and feelings about the climate crisis interfere with daily life tasks, such as eating, sleeping, and concentrating; and that jumps to an average of 70 percent for countries in the Global South. Most upsetting is the number of children who identify with some form of climate anxiety, their despair entwined with a sense of betrayal and distrust toward the grown-ups who say one thing and do another, and whose actions have done so much harm to the future. It's a widespread condition among adults as well: a 2020 poll from the American Psychiatric Association found that more than half of respondents were somewhat or extremely anxious about the impact of climate change on their own mental health. Over the past twenty years, scholars have studied more and more cases of what they call ecological grief (feelings of longing or sadness based on changes to one's ecosystem) and solastagia (feelings of nostalgia for the way one's home environment used to be).

The road to environmental doomsday in our collective mindset these days is a slick and greasy path down a very steep hill. Tallying up the disturbing evidence of the planet's decline, of youth mental health decline, of my own health decline, of geopolitical strife, of angry mobs misled by disinformation, and of countless other troubling circumstances causing wild unpredictability, doesn't take much effort. But what happens when our agitation over so much unwelcome change and unpredictability spins out?

Communities of support have emerged in response to the growing state of eco-anxiety. The Climate Psychiatry Alliance and Climate Psychology Alliance are networks of therapists whose specialties include counselling clients through the depression and paralysis that can come with overwhelming feelings of despair for the planet and our future.

Leslie Davenport is a climate psychology educator based in Washington state and the author of several books with titles like *Emotional Resiliency in the Era of Climate Change* and *What to Do When You're Worried About the Earth*. Her approach to such a complex problem is fairly straightforward: practical strategies for living a more eco-harmonious life combined with therapeutic tools for coping with the scary feelings. Acknowledge those feelings, identify them, then decide which parts of the problem you can actually do something about, and take action. It's a familiar theme: we must learn to become more comfortable in uncertainty.

Unlike some sources of stress, eco-anxiety is not imaginary—it's not about false evidence appearing real. The uncertainty about climate change is, in some respects, utterly certain: our home planet is legitimately and irreparably damaged. Toxic particulates are in my lungs. Right. Now. The challenge is to feel the discomfort without becoming overwrought. The agitated climate-fear state of mind can become myopic; we create a world view in which the feedback loop is exclusively negative and self-perpetuating. And when we're in that loop, we can't come up with solutions.

As Albert Einstein is reported to have said, "Problems cannot be solved by the same consciousness that created them." Creative, innovative, brave thinking cannot happen in a brain that is torqued into an anxious fury. The planet needs each one of us to have our frontal cortex working to its best capacity, in order for us to be creative and discover solutions to right the environmental ship. This is what psychologists refer to as the growth mindset. Panic and hysteria are the opposite of a growth mindset; they fall into the category of unproductive worry. Productive worry is what makes you book a doctor's appointment to have a lump examined, or check the weather conditions before a long drive. Unproductive worry serves no purpose and never allows for constructive and creative thinking.

Innovation can only come to a clear head—a mind that is alert and open to possibilities. This may sound Pollyannaish, but it's backed up by science. Anthony Leiserowitz and Sarah Lowe, psychologists and climate anxiety researchers at Yale University, point out that there is a significant difference between worry and anxiety. Worrying about the changing climate and our imperilled earth is a good thing. Worry is a motivating emotion; it leads us to take action. Letting that worry tip over into anxiety can be paralyzing, serving neither us nor the planet whose future we fear for. But there can be value in experiencing climate-related distress, as researchers observed in the medical journal *The Lancet*:

"Recognizing that emotions are often what leads people to act, it is possible that feelings of ecological anxiety and grief, although uncomfortable, are in fact the crucible through which humanity must pass to harness the energy and conviction that are needed for the lifesaving changes now required."

It's an entirely different way to look at change; the difference between viewing it passively as something that happens to us, versus an active approach, engaging in a conscious and proactive effort to steer the change somewhere positive. Collective action, the Yale research shows, is the most beneficial way to mitigate climate anxiety. Joining a group of like-minded concerned citizens can have a remarkably powerful effect. We know how much well-being is connected to feeling part of a community. Individual actions—like blue-bin recycling and driving an electric car—may be valuable single choices that do contribute to helping the planet, but they won't have the same impact on well-being as taking part in a larger initiative. The researchers found that the social connections and sense of communal purpose that come with a collective effort mitigate climate anxiety in a significant way.

In his 2023 book *Surviving Our Catastrophes*, psychiatrist Robert Jay Lipton explains how, in every mass trauma of the last century—Hiroshima, the Holocaust, the AIDS crisis—the formula for recovery and healing has been to come together in widespread social action. And it is precisely those who have suffered and survived whose imagination leads the way. Lipton describes the harrowing experiences of *hibakusha*—the surviving victims of the atomic bombs dropped on Hiroshima and Nagasaki—in the years following the Second World War. Their struggles after encountering so much death ultimately led to significant survivor activism, including powerful anti-nuclear protests and lasting initiatives for peace.

In the case of the climate crisis, it is the environmental scientists' commitment to facing inconvenient truths, and documenting and demonstrating the severe dangers of global warming, that has led to a shift in our awareness—what Lipton calls a "climate swerve." Resilience and renewal, he argues, can happen only when a society looks its tragedies in the eye and adapts in order to prevail. A protean attitude, open to change and movement, is the way forward; we must make the choice to adapt if we are to be resilient. Collective proteanism allows us to remain engaged with traumatic circumstances, and at the same time contribute to our recovery. The alternative, as Lipton has observed in his seven decades of psychiatric study, is stasis or fixation with what "should" be instead of what is. And there's that recurring theme when it comes to managing all of life's uncertainties: the radical acceptance of hard things.

The Good Grief Network is a non-profit that operates globally to help people struggling with anxiety over the growing climate crisis come together and turn those feelings into productive action, turning *what if* into *I can*. In their "Ten Steps to Resilience and Empowerment in a Chaotic Climate" program, the first critical step is facing the feelings. Terrifying and sweat-inducing though they may be, we need to identify our fears about the climate crisis and start to talk about them. Stewing in our heads and worrying alone don't count as action.

There is no getting past angsty feelings about global warming. Nothing about climate change will get better in our lifetime, so those feelings aren't something to be dispensed with or moved on from. Britt Wray argues one way to deal with eco-anxiety is to slow down and be curious about it. "Letting those feelings in forces us to face the problem and to stay with it." The fear, of course, is that those feelings will overwhelm us and take away our joy. But, as Wray points out, the more we avoid the self-preservation instinct that wants us to ignore the problem and pretend it will go away on its own, the more we "take away the parts of ourselves that can be responsible right now. The ability to sit with those emotions and allow them to be there is actually crucial to climate action at all."

Interestingly, in poring over the research into awe for an earlier chapter in this book, I found a study that showed a direct correlation between positive ecological behaviour and a state of awe. Feeling awe increased participants' willingness to make self-sacrifices for the environment, something the researchers attributed to the power of awe to humble us and reduce our sense of entitlement and social dominance. As they wrote of their findings, published in *Frontiers in Psychology*, "Awe mitigates the pervading belief in human hierarchical dominance over nature, which in turn increases the likelihood to act on environmental issues."

As Dacher Keltner explains in his book on awe, standing in wonder at anything that transcends our small self actually deactivates the default mode network in our brains, that habitual and unconscious pattern of being self-absorbed. Meanwhile, Shelley Carson's research at Harvard shows that one of the quickest ways to activate cognitive disinhibition—the open and aware brain state most conducive to creativity and problem-solving—is to go for a walk in the beauty of nature. Being bombarded by the extrasensory stimuli of a lush forest or a stretch of pebbled beach defocuses our attention and opens our minds to new stimuli and novel ways of thinking. And, of course, pausing to observe the earth's complexities and interconnectedness allows us to marvel at something that is bigger than us but also intimately and essentially inseparable from us. Nature offers up glimpses of beauty and meaning and grace and humbling majesty every minute of every day, and yet it owes us nothing. It just is.

What can we learn from that?

Allowing ourselves time to appreciate nature will inevitably foster a transcendent sense of wonder along with a grounding humility. Humility, lest you bristle at the notion, is often misunderstood as a lack of self-esteem; it is in fact the opposite. The Latin root of the word is *humilitas*, a noun derived from the adjective *humilis*, which translates to "grounded" or "from the earth." No amount of material achievement or technological advancement can ever separate us from the natural world. Pretending we are superior or in some way disconnected from the environment requires a uniquely human—and short-sighted—combination of ignorance and arrogance.

Humility is a strength. It is about recognizing when something is not working and having the courage to say so—not from a place of righteousness and judgment, but with a grounded purpose. We need to own up to our part in messing up the earth, and show a willingness to alter our behaviour. That's twenty-first-century courage, right there.

Change is needed in our relationship to a planet whose resources are not bottomless, and whose systems are desperately crying out for care and respect. What other choice do we have in the face of climate disaster? The options are to carry on in denial, or to continue to live in paralyzing fear, or to admit there is a problem and be courageous enough to take the action required to address it. We can numb ourselves with the blue pill of the Matrix, or face the harsh truths of what is really happening. *Take the red pill, Neo.*

"People need to feel the discomfort; it needs to break through the psychological defences that allow people to pretend themselves away from difficult truths and from a scary reality," Wray says. She makes the case that our collective eco-anxiety, that shared looming dread, can be harnessed for good. But we can't get there without first facing up to our fears.

~

Protectively seated indoors, masked to limit my particulate intake on this June afternoon, I ache for how different a world I wanted my children to grow up in; for the very real threats to the survival of life on Earth. This is happening.

It is real. Denying it is foolish and dangerous; ignoring it is impossible. There is no moving past it. I must be present for it. Sometimes sitting with uncertainty feels like hell.

In the same way that being lost forces our minds open to new details and possibilities around us, catastrophe demands that we face deeply unpalatable truths. Robert Jay Lipton argues that we must blow open the limits of our imagination for the sake of survival. We have to hold that end-of-the-world imagery close, and use it as fuel for resourcefulness. Though that's easier said than done.

I try to sit squarely with this sense of terrifying uncertainty and break it down: I fear for the impact of the particulate matter on my lungs, on my children's lungs, on the lung tissue of people I've never met. I fear for the toll this public respiratory assault will take on the already overburdened healthcare system. How do I sit with watching countless people suffer? I am enraged at all the cries for action that have been ignored for decades, by governments, business leaders, and individuals. I am terrified for the future, as wildfires become ever more common in these increasingly hot, dry summers. I mourn for how much I will miss feeling joy. What does a smoke-filled future look like? What will happen to all the children who grow up in fear? What if there's no more clean water? What if I can't breathe? Will it hurt? None of this is what any of us want. How do I adjust to this reality?

Those are the fears and questions running through my mind—a *rat-a-tat-tat* of speculation and trepidation. I try to sit with those feelings, to be present for all the fretful thinking. What do I need to learn from this painful time? What motivation might it spark? What sort of change can I try to become part of? I find that even the possibility of having some agency amid this crisis creates a shift—gives me some breathing space.

When faced with any uncertainty, pushing ourselves outside our own perspective is restorative. Helping someone or something else is therapeutic on every level. It is an extraordinary feeling to take action to solve a problem—to create something new in the face of adversity. The greater the adversity, the bigger the opportunity.

And there is, I notice, as I sit still trying to be fully present and aware of all the possibilities in this climate crisis, also birdsong. Sweet, charming trills and warbles outside the window. I cannot see its source, but the sound rings clear through the hazy morning and offers some comfort. It is not outright salvation. But it's something. Something to fight for.

Uncertainty, syn.: *Worry*

My sinus headaches have returned, tingles cascading across my scalp, as though they never left. But they actually did. For a few glorious weeks I was able, I noticed with delight one day, to move about without wearing a toque. The cozy brown beanie I had been wearing constantly, even to bed, sat limply on a chair. I no longer needed its warmth to batter the chilly ache in my head; wasn't relying on it to protect me from the slightest draft. The skull shivers and accompanying sinus headache seemed to have abated, and I had the temerity to believe I might be getting better.

Yet here I sit again, on a warm day, sporting that woollen hat—as necessary as it is ridiculous. The illusion of returning to health has faded. I can't help but feel rejected: health stopped by and rang my bell but ran away laughing when I answered the door. It will be back, I tell myself. I want to believe that feeling some symptoms abate is proof that they can—and will—again, next time for good perhaps. I try to maintain that optimism, to soak up the end-of-spring sunshine and all the hope it promises. But hope feels hard when your head hurts; when everyone else is wearing straw hats and you're the sad sack in a toque. It feels like being abandoned by a lover you had thought might be the one.

I dream of swimming. Every muscle in my body pulling together in a coordinated flow. Loose, flexible, free, strong; I am electric, and I am in motion.

FLYING BY THE SEAT OF OUR PANTS

Uncertainty is the only certainty there is, and knowing how to live with insecurity is the only security.

—John Allen Paulos

IN 1991, WITH JUST four weeks to go before defending her doctoral dissertation on early childhood linguistic development, Anne Lederer bid farewell to her fellow PhD candidates at the University of Pennsylvania and dropped out of academia. She moved to Billings, Montana, got married, and started a new chapter. Her brother, Howard Lederer, was a professional poker player—a game he and his siblings had learned at home and played for fun when they were younger. After her move to Montana, Howard encouraged Anne to take poker playing more seriously. He sent her some books on techniques, coached her on the rules and strategy over the telephone, and loaned her $2,400 to get her game going.

She got her game going, alright. Today, Annie Duke is

known as the Duchess of Poker. By the time she retired from playing professionally in 2012, she had racked up dozens of victories at various tournaments—including the World Series of Poker Tournament of Champions—and her lifetime winnings totalled well over $4 million. She is close to the top of the list of the most successful female poker players in history. (She also returned to the University of Pennsylvania in 2022 to complete her PhD.)

Duke is a self-described uncertainty evangelist. Uncertainty is of course fundamental to the game of poker—laying your chips on the table based entirely on instinct and the likelihood of an opponent's bluff is a high-stakes play, a great risk that comes with no guarantees. When that river card is flipped, and fate weighs in on whatever calculations and assumptions led to your bet, the wheel of fortune can spin as easily for you as against you. Duke's story perhaps makes earning millions at the poker table sound easy, but of course the more accurate picture of seeking one's fortune in cards is filled with many smaller victories and a huge amount of crushing debt and loss. Gambling can be as addictive as it is uncertain.

Poker, as easy as it might appear, is an incredibly complicated game. "The more you learn about poker," Duke said in an interview, "the more you realize that you don't know very much about the game, so there's an expansion of your knowledge of what you don't know as you go through." The more you realize how little you know, she argues, the better you get.

That seems like unlikely humility from someone who has mastered the game, but here, too, humility is a critical strength. Just as the arrogance of believing life should follow a plan that best suits us renders us less capable of managing change, and the grounded humility of understanding our place in nature is essential for navigating the climate crisis, being humble may well be the reason for Duke's success at the poker table. The feeling that the cards are in their favour and Lady Luck has their back has led many a card player to a haunting defeat, as the hubris of certainty overrides grounded patience and cool-headed strategy.

There is a growing body of research on the psychology of humility, as a character trait and in terms of its ties to well-being. Humility requires an accurate assessment of one's character, an awareness of one's limitations, keeping one's achievements in perspective, and appreciating other people and other ideas. Researchers refer to someone who exhibits humility as having low "self-focus" and high "other-focus." Studies suggest that people who are more humble tend to enjoy better physical and mental health than individuals who are less humble.

I had a lesson in the importance of humility on a family vacation in California, when my adolescent middle son asked to take a surf lesson. All three of my boys are lean, agile athletes for whom mastering sports comes easily; the kind of people who make coordination look obvious, and bull's eyes and smooth landings seem inevitable. They take to new activities quickly, with instincts like Hermes; teaching those boys to ride a bicycle without training wheels took less than an hour. When it comes to grace and strength, my sons do not—to be clear—take after their mother.

Lulled by the charms of surf-town culture and the groovy ease with which surfers up and down the beach rode shimmering foamy crests of one glorious wave after another, I decided I would join in—forgetting which parent had gifted my children their athletic genes. I had the core of a longtime yogi, I reassured myself with unwarranted confidence as I straddled the wide board, and the balance to go with it.

The tanned dude teaching the lesson imparted what sounded like easy advice for simple steps to follow: Paddle. Pop up. Lean in. Don't look down. There were no balls involved, no hand-eye coordination required. This might be my sport, I reasoned as I paddled a few feet offshore. In a burst of wild overconfidence, I had a sudden fantasy of all the surfing trips we could take as a family, chasing waves and hanging ten together—until the reality of my current windmill-armed fiasco drowned those delusions. I was too busy assuming I could do this incredibly hard thing to pay attention to all the steps I needed to take in order to pull it off. Possibly the most futile undertaking of my adult life, my surfing lesson was brief and unforgettable: an inelegant series of spectacular, flailing spills in knee-deep waves. A textbook kook, in true surfer parlance. I remain humbled by all that I don't know, and will likely never know, about how to surf.

Why does pride usually come before a fall? When we allow ourselves to feel certainty, we become closed-minded. Assumptions shut us off from other possibilities, from learning or observing new information, from staying curious and updating our beliefs to adapt to change. When we lean on certainty, we aren't motivated to be resourceful.

Metaphorically and physically, surfing is the ultimate manifestation of navigating uncertainty. Paying attention to the immediacy of the moment, accepting what comes with humility and curiosity, and letting go of assumptions about what should happen. That's the chestnut of meditative wisdom from mindfulness pioneer Jon Kabat-Zinn. A professor emeritus at the University of Massachusetts Medical School, Kabat-Zinn is the founder of the widely prescribed Mindfulness Based Stress Reduction (MBSR) program, and the author of fifteen books that have been translated into forty-five languages. Of all his lasting accomplishments, he is perhaps best known for the simple axiom of modern living that distills everything he teaches into a single sentence: "You can't stop the waves, but you can learn to surf."

And that's what this entire inquiry around handling uncertainty all boils down to, isn't it? Figuring out how to stay emotionally afloat in a tsunami of change.

~

On a clear evening in early January 1999, a team of NASA scientists at Space Launch Complex 17B at Cape Canaveral in Florida said *au revoir* to a 290-kilogram spacecraft known as the Mars Polar Lander as they sent it hurtling into space. They had high hopes. The lander was part of the Mars Surveyor '98 program; this little roving probe, three metres wide with retractable aluminium legs and a honeycomb of solar panels on its back, would be the first spacecraft ever to beam back images of the surface of the red planet. And not just any part of the surface. The Martian south pole was widely suspected to be the location of a large section of frozen water buried beneath a thin layer of dust. The Mars Polar Lander's mission, with a price tag of $165 million, was to land safely in the Planum Australe region of the south pole, search for near-surface ground ice, and analyze the soil for physically and chemically bound carbon dioxide and water.

This was big, even outside space science circles. Between all the extraterrestrial believers, the generally curious, and the more than one million children from around the world whose signatures were burned onto a CD-ROM put onboard the lander as part of the "Send Your Name to Mars" campaign, there was a lot of buzz about this mission and an eager anticipation of all that it would deliver.

For the science news program I hosted at the Discovery Channel at the time, this was basically the Academy Awards. Bring on the pomp, the live special, and the travel budget. My co-presenter Jay Ingram and I were sent to California for a few days of interviews, and to prep ahead of the three-hour network-wide live special we would host. Jay and I each ran around Los Angeles with our assigned producers filming interviews to use as set-up during the show while we waited for the live images to begin transmitting.

I recorded an interview with Gary Sinise, star of the upcoming *Mission to Mars* movie—because really, what serious space enthusiast doesn't want to hear from a Hollywood star who has, well, worn a space suit, about what it felt like to walk on the fake Martian landscape created by a team of set decorators? I also visited the Hollywood set of the film *Red Planet*, then in production, and taped an interview with Benjamin Bratt (clearly I was on the handsome-actors-pretending-to-be-space-explorers-onscreen beat when it came to our pre-show prep)—capturing the excitement the world was feeling about Mars and its infinite possibilities on the cusp of a new millennium.

The big day arrived. December 3, 1999. The Discovery Channel field crew was assembled at NASA's Jet Propulsion Laboratory in Pasadena. Our dry run-throughs complete, Jay and I were positioned on our temporary set under a large white tent protecting us from the late-afternoon Californian sun. A giant television monitor stood between our stools so we could point specifically to the Mars surface images on which the NASA analysts would be commenting. Together with the world, in real time, we would discover what it really looked like on Mars.

The thrilling prospect of witnessing such a historic scientific breakthrough added an extra frisson to the live-show countdown. The special animated graphics rolled, and we began to recite our prepared introductions. There was no teleprompter on this remote camera set-up; we had nothing but a few cue cards and rehearsed talking points and our natural curiosity to go on. Jay and I bantered enthusiastically for a while, talking over graphics of the landing site. We explained to the audience that there would be a six-minute communication dropout as the capsule entered Mars's orbit, its heat shield blocking signals as it absorbed the thousand-plus-degree temperatures while passing through the planet's atmosphere.

Eventually, our buzzy build-up to the big moment complete, the appointed juncture arrived and the landing sequence began. We bantered some more about how the three-legged landing system would work, and how the spacecraft's probes would penetrate the Martian soil to study its subsurface.

After what felt like much longer than six minutes, the show director cued in Jay's ear to introduce the Gary Sinise interview. We were officially filling time. But we were prepared for this. It wasn't unreasonable that a broadcast signal from 95 million miles away in space would have a bit of a transmission lag. No problem. As the pre-recorded item rolled to air and our microphones were muted, we joked aloud about having over two and a half hours left of our much-hyped live national broadcast special to fill, and could the Mars Polar Lander please start sending some images back, any minute now, to give us something to talk about. We laughed easily, confident that this historic, multimillion-dollar feat of engineering would deliver on its promise and begin transmitting images from the planet's surface any minute.

But it never did. No further signals were received from the spacecraft. For anyone not tracking the math, that left my co-host and me with approximately 150 minutes of airtime to fill and *literally nothing to talk about*.

No one yet understood what had happened—the disaster was unfolding in real time. How many ways are there to say that a mission has failed? What on earth would we report on for two and a half more hours of live television? What could we possibly say? Our hard-working producers scrambled behind the scenes to find analysts for us to interview to explain what had happened, but no one seemed to know much. The NASA engineers were doing their own racing around in control centres all over the Jet Propulsion Lab, shaking their heads, palms held over brows, trying desperately to understand what had gone wrong. (The Mars Polar Lander would eventually be classified as a failed mission, categorized as lost on arrival. It has never been spotted by subsequent rovers and remains lost to this day.)

Our rehearsals, plans, and groundwork were no longer relevant as we were thrust headlong into immediacy. In the middle of this crisis of uncertainty, getting caught up in the why-is-this-happening narrative—a classic step in the rush to panic—usually feels like a natural first instinct; and yet it serves no purpose. Even if we had been able to wrangle the one aeronautical engineer who could pinpoint the error in impact velocity calculations, that might have satisfied the space exploration enthusiasts but it wouldn't have solved more than about five minutes of the roughly two-hour problem of being stuck on a commercial-free live broadcast with no backup plan. To ask why something has gone wrong is to waste time scrambling in frustration and wanting out of the moment. There's usually a time for reflecting on errors made and choices that could have led to a different outcome, but that comes later. In the moment, there is, in fact, just the moment.

When the wheels have literally fallen off but the show must go on, what do you do? There is no script, no certainty, and no escape. (There was also, by that point, probably no audience.)

"Well, this is going to make for some gripping live television, isn't it? A show about something that didn't actually happen!" I joked—even though it wasn't a joke. But we had to laugh at ourselves. Ego, move over, there's no room for you here. We have a dripping egg of awkwardness running all over our TV-makeup faces, and there's no point in pretending otherwise.

In the end, my response to being smack in the middle of an unmitigated disaster was to ... lean into it. *This is ridiculous*, I told myself, *and everyone knows it, so it's time to acknowledge that.*

Calling out a situation with humility and candour can feel awkwardly vulnerable; it's an admission of some degree of failure. But I find (because it has happened to me on so, so many occasions, both on and off the air) it is also terribly liberating—everyone on both sides of the camera, in every aspect of the situation, is liberated from the pretence of order, of control. Of certainty. The self-deprecating habit of admitting *I'm not sure what exactly is happening* during live broadcasts is a strangely comfortable pattern for me; something about the vulnerability of it makes me feel stronger and less alone.

I gave up working in television as soon as I got the chance to get back to my roots in radio. Television has its glamorous charms, but I definitely don't miss the hours of fuss in the makeup chair. For the last fifteen years, I've worked on radio, mostly as the host of Toronto's afternoon drive show. It's a top-rated show in the country's largest market, a lively juggle of interviews covering the news of the day, with a heavy dose of arts and culture thrown into the mix. I never know what each day will bring, but it's always interesting.

A few days after taking over the job as executive producer of the program I host, my new boss sent me a quick email. She'd been observing the teams and programs that were now under her purview and she wanted to let me know about a thought she had jotted in her notebook: *Gill—high level of comfort with uncertainty*. She wasn't wrong; living with uncertainty could be a subheading on my business card. My new boss wondered what I thought about why, besides my lengthy experience as a live broadcaster, that was the case.

The uncertainty and unpredictability of content are baked into the premise of a live radio program—especially, though not uniquely, when you're broadcasting in the afternoon. So much can happen in the course of three middle-of-the-day hours. When events occur, it is a news organization's job to report the facts, parse the details, analyze the impact. On a live program, those steps happen almost instantaneously. Reacting to the news of the moment is job number one for a nimble current affairs program, and that means an unspoken contract with the unknown.

Nelson Mandela died on December 5, 2013. His death was announced on national television by then-president Jacob Zuma, shortly before midnight local time. In mere minutes, the historic news had spread around the world. I was live on the air when the story broke, in the middle of whatever programming our team had thought constituted the most important news of the day. In the blink of an eye, that standard was turned upside down, and the announcement of the death of one of my generation's most significant and revered political heroes fell to me. I threw aside the script I had been given for a planned interview about that weekend's upcoming Santa Claus parade, and instead leaned into the unscripted, unplanned moment of honouring the legendary anti-apartheid activist—the father of modern South Africa. So many emotions flooded my brain, everything felt raw and important and immediate. To experience and react to big news *at the same time as the audience* feels like rare chemistry, magnetic and unforgettable. That urgent aliveness, unstable though it is, is a gorgeous by-product of uncertainty.

The world serves up changing news for us to adapt to; then life throws in a few technical and logistical curve balls, just to keep it interesting. When the computer system crashes in the control room during a live radio show, there is only one tool left for sending content out across the airwaves: the in-studio microphone (and the host who speaks into it). At least once every couple of weeks during our three-hour radio show on the national public broadcaster, I get a signal from the technical producer on the other side of a glass wall, letting me know that the system has stopped working and she has to reboot. I keep a few tricks up my sleeve for filling time, but at a certain point the listener can tell the jig is up; there's only so much tap dancing I can do before the audience hears a hollow, pointless ramble. That's when I rely on my habit of leaning into the mess: "Well, this is interesting, our computer system has crashed. It will take a couple of minutes to get it back up and running again, but until it is, I can't play you that song I promised, so you're stuck with me. Did I mention this is live radio, folks? Anything can happen ..."

And just like that any stress I might have felt is released. I have no secrets, I cannot be held responsible for circumstances beyond my control. My vulnerability becomes a point of connection. Things haven't turned out as we had hoped or planned they would, and I feel relieved not to have to pretend otherwise.

In the theatre it's called breaking the fourth wall. If a typical stage has three walls—along the back and two sides—the fourth is the invisible one through which the audience looks; that imaginary veil in front of the performers that allows those watching to suspend their disbelief and let things unfold in whatever way has been prepared for them. Breaking the fourth wall acknowledges the pretence. David Letterman used to do it all the time during his *Late Night* talk show. He'd admit to there being a producer behind the camera frantically waving at him to do something; the screen would cut to a shot of the producer waving, then being aware they'd been captured on film doing it, and the audience was immediately in on the joke. Everyone laughed and the audience felt closer to Dave—like he was letting us all in on the mechanics of how this giant success of a show came together. Breaking down artifice and acknowledging failures when they happen are gestures of candour. And—though it might not feel like it in the moment—confidence.

In the middle of wild uncertainty, there is no shame in admitting to your struggle and calling out your uneasiness for what it is. This might seem like the hardest step to take if there is ego or pride in the way, but I think of it as the easiest. Because it's the one right in front of you.

We are socialized to believe that wisdom is knowing—that the more a person knows, the wiser they are. We put our trust in those who seem to know a lot, and we resist admitting when we don't know something. Too often, we think of not knowing and vulnerability as weaknesses. But I think we've got it backwards. Socrates said, "I know one thing—I know nothing." And maybe that's the difference between wisdom and knowledge: those that are wise can accept being lost and not knowing. That's the kind of honesty that builds trust. When you admit to all that you don't know, what you *do* know is more reliable. And being vulnerable allows opportunities to learn and grow: we can't be taught what we think we already know.

In the inexorable entropy of life, there is luck and chance involved in almost everything. We need to change our relationship to saying *I don't know*—because as Annie Duke has learned in her years at the world's most competitive poker tables, uncertainty is a much more accurate view of the way the world works. "And," she argues, "the more accurate your representation of the world, the better your decisions are and the better you're able to propel yourself to success." She attributes her success at poker to a constant calibration of all that she *doesn't know* about how the game will unfold.

The most successful leaders are comfortable with that

kind of honesty and vulnerability. Innovative and committed to core values, yes. But also able to ask for help and admit weakness. A willingness to be present and attuned to what is happening in the here and now, without needing to know all the answers and impose a plan on a situation, is magnetic—and it is a model of strength and empowerment. It allows space for others to play a role, to lean into their own potential, to feel part of the team or community.

At the end of each workday, when my husband asks me how the show went that afternoon, I usually say it was good, and maybe relay something interesting I learned. But on the days when something went wrong, I don't say it was good. I say it was awesome. Those days are the most fun, the most electric, the most memorable. When things are most uncertain, they are most alive. The beauty of unpredictability is that it can yank us out of a rut or a lifeless lull, and drag us right into the heart of the situation. We become fully present and attuned to the life we've got right now, complete with all the emotions and challenges we may not like the feel of. But we feel them anyway. As a nurse once said to me when I complained that his tugging on a post-operative drainage tube was causing me a jolt of pain, "That's how you know you are alive." I didn't appreciate the sentiment at the time, but it's a line that comes back to me when I experience something that feels difficult. Humans are born with a range of emotional capabilities and an expansive set of processing muscles; we just prefer to use the pleasurable ones.

The confidence you bring to an unpredictable or uncomfortable situation by being honest and vulnerable about what's happening may be your escape route from suffering through it. I've thought a lot about that question from my executive producer. How *did* I become so comfortable with uncertainty? Here is what I emailed her in reply:

> My glib and hasty answer, though not entirely untrue, is something to do with having had cancer 3 times. Good training for living with uncertainty ... But the bigger truth is that while I have no official training in journalism, I came up through improvisational sketch comedy theatre. I've always been drawn to the challenge and risk of uncertainty, I like having to spot and grasp a narrative as it appears. I find the mental/intellectual effort of navigating the high wire tightrope to be deeply satisfying.

Probably the absolute best way to get comfortable with uncertainty, and have a lot of fun while you're at it, is to take part in some form of improvisational sketch comedy. In any theatre class I took in high school, my favourite part was always the improv games. The Three-Headed Expert, in which a trio of players cobble together pithy answers to an arbitrary question, each only contributing one word at a time. The Gibberish game, in which players take a random prompt and act out a story using only nonsense speech. The Human Machine, in which each player in the group makes a sound and movement, contributing to a collective physical embodiment of an inanimate object, and the audience must guess what that object is. Or the game where everything in the scene must be spoken in the form of a question ... There are countless improvisational exercises, each more fun and ridiculous than the next. I loved the playfulness, the frivolity, the heady challenge of exploring with my classmates to find laughs and a story, the freedom of not having to stick to an imposed script.

In university, I joined a local troupe that put on weekly improv sketch comedy performances for a live audience. What happens in an improv sketch? The audience toss a few prompts at the performers—location, profession, time of day, or any other number of details—and the troupe on stage has to immediately pull together a compelling and hopefully comedic narrative without any preparation.

That much, you probably know.

But what is really happening in the performance of an improv sketch? The rest of the world falls entirely away. There is nothing to think about or do but listen, observe, and react to the gestures and cues and offerings of your fellow players—to find the joy, the story, the feeling, even the humour in what is right in front of you.

The fundamental principle of improvisation, the core tenet by which every performer lives and dies, is a two-word mantra: *Yes, and.* A performer never blocks or rejects what is being proposed by a fellow cast member; instead they accept (*yes*) and move it forward, embracing it and making the most of it (*and*). So the response to "How did that bird wind up on your head?" would never be "What bird?" Instead it would be something like, "Not again! This has been happening ever since I switched to a new shampoo ..." or "Oh, there it is! Let's call Mrs. Smith and tell her we've found her parakeet ..."

There is a model for life here. Pay attention to and be present for what is happening, be curious about where it might lead and humble enough not to resist when the script doesn't unfold the way you thought it should. It's how Miles Davis responded to Herbie Hancock's "wrong" notes; jazz, after all, is improv. It's how we learn to surf on the waves of life's fast-paced changes and challenges: by being present in the moment and accepting what is happening, with humility and curiosity.

Keith Johnstone, who died in early 2023 at the age of ninety, was a much-admired and internationally renowned pioneer of improvisation. Over multiple decades, he taught many thousands of students—*Kids in the Hall*'s Bruce McCulloch and Mark McKinney, *Breaking Bad* and *Better Call Saul* actor Bob Odenkirk, and *Parks and Recreation* writer Norm Hiscock among them. He was the founder of Theatresports, a widely beloved competitive style of improv performance, and counted the theatre giants Harold Pinter and Samuel Beckett among his friends. As the tributes rang out in the wake of his death, the depth of Johnstone's impact became clear. Student after student, colleague after colleague, recalled his ability to create a safe space where people could fall on their face without shame and were supported in picking themselves back up and trying again.

Johnstone spent most of his career teaching his students to become more comfortable with uncertainty. When you're on stage making up a performance as you go, the most common pitfall is for a performer to try to be extra witty and original; when in truth, the funniest and most successfully improvised moments don't come when you strive for them and swing for the comedy fences. Johnstone's message to his many students over the years was to stop looking for what is clever and instead look for what is obvious. In other words, stop trying to control what happens, and just be present for what is happening.

Our desire to control the outcome of our stories—on stages of all sizes, both physical and metaphorical—is so often what gets in the way of our ability to enjoy what's right in front of us. When we manage to be present for what is happening in the moment, and let go of our preconceived ideas of how things should go, our minds are open to possibilities we hadn't ever conceived of. On an improv stage, the results (on a good night) will seem brilliant and hilarious to the audience and exhilaratingly liberating for the performer.

Johnstone took his love of spontaneity one step further during live improv shows, reportedly advising players to try to make at least three mistakes. He had a reputation for giving feedback to lighting and technical crews after a show, saying, "You were perfect. But couldn't you have made a few mistakes?"

When have you ever been encouraged to make more mistakes in your life? Striving for perfection is a curse—presumably because it's unachievable. As Ursula K. Le Guin beautifully put it in her book *The Wave in the Mind*, "Perfectionism is our most compulsive way of keeping ourselves small, a kind of psycho emotional contortionism that gives the illusion of reaching for greatness while constricting us into increasingly suffocating smallness."

Embracing the inevitability of our mistakes and normalizing them allows us to recalibrate our relationship with failure—something many of us spend a lot of time and energy being afraid of and working to avoid.

No matter how hard we try to steer clear of it, failure is always hovering in the periphery. Of course it is—without the potential of failure, life is neutered to dullness and nothing we attempt has any stakes. The shadow of failure is right there waiting for us when we wake up in the morning, and it is inherent in every choice we make. And nowhere is that threat of failure more imminent than in a live performance with no script and no knowledge of what anyone around you might say or do. I was always too busy laughing and playing to realize it, but in that respect, improv comedy is a crash course in vulnerability and a training camp for life. An improvised performance is a series of small failures, humiliations, and indignities that are nevertheless hilarious and, more subtly, confidence-building. Each time I bounced back from a fumbled joke or an embarrassing misstep in an attempt to impersonate a microwave or speak in a Cockney accent, on some level I was shaping my own resilience—developing a tenacity in the face of hard things.

Stoicism, a philosophy of personal ethics that dates back to the third century BC, celebrates the development of resilience through experiencing adversity. In the same way a vaccine gives the body a small taste of something harmful to enable the immune system to learn to handle it, the Stoics believed in a psychological immune response. Learning to fail a little bit, to struggle and fall and get back up again, serves two purposes: first, it musses up our clothes, and reminds us that the idea that they'd stay pressed and unstained was always preposterous; and second, it builds and strengthens our get-back-up-again muscles—what we might call resilience. Improv performing is not, I'm certain, in the Stoic playbook. But it is an excellent practice for getting comfortable with mistakes, developing a new relationship with uncertainty, and establishing a foundational mindset of resilience.

Improv builds the habit of failure, helping to strip it of the unpleasantness we tend to associate with defeat. Because it's what we do with failure that matters, and how we feel about its looming presence in our daily lives. Being afraid of it leads to worry and stress; improvising declaws failure, so we can look it in the eye with a shrug. Live performance has so many imperfections baked into it that the only option is to adapt, hopefully coax a laugh out of any mistakes, and keep on keeping on.

Unscripted live performance is not for everyone, of course (though taking an improv workshop with a friend is a surefire way to make you laugh and expand your comfort zone, rearranging your relationship with uncertainty—that much I can guarantee). But there is much off-stage wisdom embedded into the architecture of improvisation: accept that a script or agenda is only ever a best-laid plan.

What I think is probably going to happen and what I plan for at work is something I never let myself grow too attached to. And by not being too attached to a plan, by expecting change—in fact, not only expecting it but *valuing* that change—I am freed up to be receptive and present for all that it entails. The key is to listen acutely, and to squeeze the vitality out of any given moment. Uncertainty creates space for new information. Like new blood, adding oxygen.

Somebody on the NASA team involved in the Mars Polar Lander mission may have made a mistake; an expensive error that caused a lot of people a lot of anguish that December day in 1999. I don't know whether the technical malfunction was the result of human error or some unforeseeable extraplanetary force that prevented the mission from going as planned. But you can be sure that team of scientists learned from their very public failure. Drawing boards were returned to, calculations were fine-tuned, research schedules were adjusted. Clearly the mistakes made and their inherent lessons held value: since then, several successful Mars exploration rovers have landed with full function. Who knows by what process those missions are named, but their monikers seem significant in the context of riding the wave of uncertainty: Spirit (2004), Opportunity (2004), Phoenix (2008), Curiosity (2012), and Perseverance (2021).

As for the live broadcast that evening, I can't say for sure how interesting the Discovery Channel programming was to audiences here on Earth. What I do know is that I got a valuable surfing lesson right there on dry land in Pasadena. Take whatever comes, stay loose and open to the undulations, feel the wet spray and wind on your face, and lean into the ride.

Uncertainty, syn.: *Unpredictability*

I want to tell you the end of the story.

I want to be able to give you a happy ending. I want the happy ending, I want it for me most of all.

I want the story to be that I was sick, for a long time—so sick that I couldn't work or go to the grocery store or talk on the telephone. That I was sick and that there were no answers and there were countless doctors' appointments and my family was worried and my body hurt in weird ways that made no sense to anyone, and I lay down more than I stood up and I doubted whether I'd ever get better and I cried in the bathtub after the final episode of *Derry Girls*, overwhelmed by envy for the people out in the world able to make things, tell stories, live big lives, harness their energy to make their ideas and dreams come into being, and I felt so sorry for myself because the prospect of doing anything interesting outside these four walls seemed over and the possibility of my existence being measured in any way beyond answering queries of "How are you feeling today?" seemed extinguished.

Maybe we could craft the narrative so it builds up to a singular dramatic dark moment—the crisis climax in the story when all seemed lost. Maybe I'd step out of the bathtub, dripping tears and tepid bathwater, towel myself off, and curl up sadly under my covers for what felt like the ten millionth time, only that time I would be thinking dark thoughts and for the first time in my life wondering if I could continue to live like this, if a life without energy and activity held enough meaning to be worth keeping on with. Perhaps I'd lie there, imagining it all coming to an end, but then remembering that I loved my children too much to ever leave them prematurely and that I owed them my presence to bear witness to their own glorious lives and to watch their dreams unfold. And I would think that maybe this wasn't the end of life altogether but more the end of my youth—the period when I had agency, the time my father used to call the juice years. Maybe I would think it was time to make peace with decline; to surrender any personal ambition; to tally up my life's worth with more of a backwards glance than a forward one. I've had a good run and now I'll hang back and watch from the sidelines, I would think, understanding that this was just what it's like to be at the end of life. And slowly, with an uneasy peace descending over me, coupled with the muscular release from the Epsom salt–filled bath, I would drift off to sleep.

Dawn would come, as it does in every story. And as it broke, the camera would find me rubbing my eyes and awakening to birdsong, the scene lit with the sweet sunshine of a May day that brings hope to a morning. I would step out of bed and begin my day, and sometime in the midst of the ordinary tasks that made up my reduced life, I would notice that I didn't have a headache, that the throbbing feeling in my sinus cavity hadn't acted up yet. I would eat food without digestive consequence. Maybe my phone would ring and I'd realize I had left it by my bed, and I would bound up the stairs to grab it and suddenly notice I had stair-bounding energy today. The active feat would pump wind into my sails; I'd catch my reflection in the mirror and smile at the woman I used to know. And that evening I would be kinder to my family; no torturous headache would be gripping my skull and neck and draining all affection from my being. Someone would turn up the music and I wouldn't have to leave the room covering my ears; instead, I'd stand up and dance, feeling sensual whispers of motion pass easily through my muscles and joints. I would be able to stay awake long enough to embrace my husband when he came to bed, wrap myself around him and love him the way I wanted to. And after a few days of this insouciant aliveness, I would cautiously dare to hope I was better; after a few weeks of so much liveliness, I would feel like a space traveller in zero gravity and know that the weight of what had seemed like an eternal illness was well and truly gone. I would see friends, answer my phone, run errands, bake a cake. I would go back to work. I would hug colleagues whose laughter I had missed, look them in the eye and thank them for their patience with me, then hug them one more time by way of apology for how challenging it must have been to have to work around the uncertainty of my absence for so long.

I would visit my lonely mother. I would plant a garden. I would sing. I would say yes to things that lifted my heart. And as the camera pulls back on the widening shot of me marching down the street, destination anywhere, I would kick up my heels.

Fade to black.

That is how I want this story to end. Writing it down feels so good I almost don't want to stop imagining the life I used to have being real and true once more. I want to have it back. I want to hurry up and get to the part where there's a lesson in all of this, a slow-down-and-smell-the-roses kind of wisdom I'll have earned, a clarity of priorities, an epiphanic shift of never taking a spring in my step for granted ever again. I'll learn the lesson, I swear—just let me have my health back.

I wish I could push past the uncomfortable parts of right now, the immediate this, cruise through the dark and rough-edged tunnel with my hands squarely planted over my ears—I wish I could make this all go away so I can get back to the good stuff. Even the hard stuff would be better, as long as it wasn't like *this*.

But I'm here. And it is this. The immediate *this*. It's really all we ever have.

PRO TEMPORE

There is nothing permanent except change.
—*Heraclitus*

SOMEONE HAS SENT YOU flowers to mark a special occasion. As you place the cut stems in a vase, admiring their colourful burst of fragrant cheer, you know, in spite of not wanting to believe this exuberant glory will ever fade, that in a matter of days these gorgeous blooms will brown, wilt, and droop. The water that nourishes the stems will grow cloudy and stale, ceasing to be enough to sustain the delicate petals. Just as you know that every time you pull weeds from the garden, or sweep up dust clusters from under the bed, they'll be back. The pristine state of your tended flower bed, your cleanly wiped table, your freshly washed car, your tidy bedroom is, of course, temporary.

The second law of thermodynamics says that all natural processes run in one direction only. Energy disperses and systems dissolve. That's why the ice cubes in your glass of water will never not melt, your beloved pet will never grow less old, that newly repaired drywall will never not settle, shift, and one day form a crack at the seam, your body will never become less inclined toward degeneration. Disintegration cannot be avoided. Nature and time charge a tax on everything: chemistry, economics, climate, weather systems. Weeds of some sort will always overtake the proverbial garden. Dust is collecting on your furniture even as you read this. Your mug of steaming tea will lose its heat and grow cold, likely before you remember to drink it. Every entity is constantly moving toward decay and disorder. Entropy is inevitable. And it always increases with the passage of time.

Systems tend toward increasing disorder and will eventually devolve into disarray. Chaos is everywhere.

How much is your struggle with uncertainty rooted in the belief that you're supposed to be in control of how things go? That the right amount of striving and planning and vigilance and mitigating unwelcome change will keep your life on the path to whatever outcome you seek? I would wager it's a lot. That belief, delusional though it may be, is one most of us share. It's how our ordered, measured, reward-for-effort society conditions us to operate. But as anyone who has hit a rocky patch along the way can tell you, the notion of having control over our lives is an illusion. And clinging to that illusion only makes us less prepared for the inevitable hardships when they occur.

The first time I was diagnosed with cancer (not the way anyone wants to start a sentence), I was forty-two. My husband, Grant, and I were living in Toronto with our three small children, all boys. Our family was complete—we felt clear on that. Years before, when our son Harper was about eighteen months old, I'd started to have a sense that we should have a third child. Grant and I had never consciously envisioned a certain size family—we're not terribly good planners, at least not insofar as scripting big life events far in advance; we usually operate by gut feel. But that gut had started to tell me in a loud voice that there was someone else waiting to arrive—another person our family needed. And we did need Miles, who was born a year later. After that, I didn't hear a call for any new members for our tribe. (To be honest, I might not have been able to hear much at all over the din of three-boy mayhem.)

So, in early 2009, just before I found that lump in my breast, I was feeling pretty good, pretty comfortable in the easy assurance that things were unfolding as they should—*should* according to what or whom, I don't know, but at the time it felt like I was the architect of something and I liked what I was building. My youngest child was out of diapers, my career as a television and radio broadcaster was … okay, admittedly a hodge-podge freelance juggle. But still. I had work opportunities, ideas, energy, and hope. And a house full of happy, healthy, delightful little ragamuffins. Sometimes when I'd come home after dusk, stepping into my backyard through the rear gate off our neighbourhood alley, I would look up at the objectively unimpressive rear view of my home and be struck with an overwhelming sense of fulfillment. I saw my slightly crooked house—its exterior in need of a paint job, the small yard cluttered with bicycles—lit up from within; a peek at the warmth of home. From where I stood in the fading light, I couldn't see the mess or the squabbles that awaited my attention inside; all I could see was the nest Grant and I had made for our clan. We had a home and a healthy family. My heart swelled with the blessings.

But beyond blessings, if I'm honest, I felt a little *satisfied*, like my choices and efforts had been validated. I thought I was adhering to some time-honoured narrative of how to properly play the game of life. A home with three young children was invariably a little chaotic, but at least I had *some* things under control. I was a runner, a yogi, and a vegetarian. I tried to cook organic food and limit the toxic chemical ingredients we came into contact with. I thought ahead, did the research, went the extra precautionary mile to make our home a healthy one. And it seemed like all that hard work had paid off. I was on track—following not so much a plan as an assumption about the way the world should be.

It was around that time that the freelance juggle I called a career offered up an opportunity to take a little trip down the Amazon. This particular work assignment had Grant and me on a large boat travelling through the jungle of Peru. After a few days of sticky, tropical, near unbearable heat, I cheekily suggested a swim. Yes, in the Amazon, waters that are chock full of anacondas and piranhas. Looming threats. *No one swims here*, our guide cautioned us. Undeterred, I plunged in, terrified at first and then quickly overcome with cooling relief. Carefree, feeling bold, I returned to our cabin a little frisky. But mid-fondle, our holiday passions were suddenly iced by Grant's discovery of what felt like a chickpea in the tissue of my left breast. It was hard, new, and definitely unfamiliar.

Three weeks later, I was getting a mammogram. Then, suddenly, and almost immediately, being whisked into another room and told I needed a biopsy and was I available … now? How about now? Like, immediately. *Do you have a person? A husband? Call him, you'll want him to take you home, you'll be sore.* Wait, what? My first-ever mammogram and I didn't even get to make a panini-press joke. I jumped straight to the stab in the breast with a knitting needle, also known as a punch biopsy. I have no memory of receiving the diagnosis a week later.

A cancer diagnosis comes loaded with the full menu of fear-based uncertainties—existential terrors that slam hard into the presumption of health. How naive I was, poor thing, thinking that I had any right to expect all my best-laid plans for health and harmony to unfold as I wanted them to. I'd been trying to adhere to a presumed path, a controlled outcome, straining to keep discord and strife at bay. But how wrong I was to imagine that a full life could ever be lived without fear, pain, and uncertainty. All of us, if we're honest, are defenceless against the vagaries of the world.

A cancer diagnosis is a lot of things, nearly all of them devastating. But if there is one possible blessing offered up in the shitstorm, it is having to accept the wobbliness of being alive, learning to walk side by side with suffering, stand comfortably in the same room with unknowing, and let go of control—or of the illusion of ever having had it in the first place. Less-mortal terrors often drive us to cling more intently to the sweet promise of control, to grasp desperately at what was and what has been, to try to rush through the challenge and whisk ourselves back to a comfortable stasis. But a cancer diagnosis refuses to be ignored. To wish it away is to be in an argument with reality. Preconceived ideas and accepted conventions about how your life is going to go evaporate in the same breath your doctor expends in relaying the bad news. Terror takes over. The body is flooded with panic, worry, and dread. As those feelings percolate, different flavours bubble to the surface: anger, determination, maybe regret. There's a surge of grit, the fiery intention to get answers, make decisions, move swiftly to solve the problem. To move through the uncertainty as fast as possible. There is the powerful impulse to hang on, white-knuckled, to what was and what has been.

Eventually we begin to smell other ingredients in the emotional stew, delicate flavours that are hard to taste at first. For me, one of them was surrender. I never abandoned my determination to remove the cancer from my body and do whatever it took to lessen the chance of it ever coming back; there are late-stage cancer diagnoses when time has in fact run out, and I can only imagine the harrowing and painful challenge for both patient and family of surrendering to the end of a precious life. But in so many treatable cases, the surrender is not to cancer itself but to a different kind of disease: the human condition of needing to be on top. To know what is happening and why.

What is happening? How much will it hurt? When does this

end? Who will I be when it's over? A team of oncologists called upon their best instincts and decades of experience to guide my treatment, and gave me their most sincere predictions of a hopeful outcome. But the illusion that I could ever have the answers, or know what tomorrow held, was forever shattered. There was nothing left to do but find a new appreciation of what I already had. Written into the fine stitches of the long mastectomy scar that now meandered across my chest in place of my left breast was a message about how to live differently: *Today is all you get. Make sure you're here for it.*

Amanda Knox was twenty years old when she went to prison for a crime she did not commit. In 2007, during an undergraduate year abroad in Italy, Amanda was sharing a cottage apartment near the University for Foreigners of Perugia with a few fellow students—including Meredith Kercher, another American spending the year abroad. Returning home one day to find blood in the bathroom and Meredith's bedroom door locked, Amanda called the police. When Meredith was found dead in her room, Amanda was the first to be interviewed by the Italian authorities. For a total of fifty-three hours over the course of five days, her interrogations continued—in Italian, a language in which she was not yet proficient. She was eventually coerced into signing papers she didn't understand, mistakenly implicating herself in the crime. She spent two years in prison awaiting trial, vilified as a sex-crazed murderer by the media and mistreated by prison guards, counting the days until she could clear her name and be liberated from her nightmare.

In 2009, after a trial that featured hapless detectives, impatient prosecutors, and so much confusion that international observers called it a wild miscarriage of justice, Knox was not, in fact, released as she had assumed she would be. Convicted for the murder of Meredith Kercher, she was sentenced to twenty-six years in prison. International media attention and intervention from US forensic experts ultimately disproved the state's case. A local burglar was convicted of the murder after his bloodstained fingerprints were found on Kercher's possessions. In 2011, Knox was freed from prison and returned home to the United States. But it wasn't until 2015 that she was officially exonerated by Italy's highest court.

What do we do with news that is as devastating as it is unfair? How do we face the days ahead when they are stripped of the order, predictability, comfort, and hope we thought we deserved? In 2023, Knox shared a series of posts on Twitter (now X) describing an epiphany that overcame her on the day of her verdict in 2009—the day she had thought she would be freed but was instead sentenced to twenty-six years of incarceration. "I'd thought I was in limbo, awkwardly positioned between my life (the life I should have been living), and someone else's life (the life of a murderer). I wasn't. I never had been. The conviction, the sentence, the prison cell—*this* was my life. There was no life I *should* have been living. There was only my life, this life, unfolding before me."

This moment, this one right now as you read these very words—can you feel it? Buddhists say that it's all we have, that the present moment is all that is real. Everything that has already happened exists only in memory, and everything you think should or will happen is simply that—a thought, a projection of the future.

Psychologists and therapists call the surrender to the present moment, no matter what hardships it may contain, radical acceptance—this is the complete recognition and acceptance of the reality in which we find ourselves, even when that reality includes pain and discomfort. Even when that reality is inherently uncertain and colossally unfair. In the face of something as inescapable as a cancer diagnosis or a death, an irretrievable loss or the iron bars of a prison cell, ignoring and avoiding are no longer options. To spend time resisting that reality, wishing that the situation were anything other than what it is, grieving the life we thought we should have been living instead, just adds to our suffering. Stewing over uncertainty makes a tense situation worse. It's like creating another prison within the difficult circumstances you're already in.

Radical acceptance is not a giving up, not an approval or a defeated shoulder shrug in the face of hard things. Radical acceptance is a conscious effort to honour and acknowledge a difficult situation. It is part of the cognitive behavioural therapy model of increasing one's tolerance for distress, in order to help keep pain from turning into suffering. And it works for everyday challenges, as well as life-and-death ones.

A friend who works in the film and television industry

told me about a particularly gruelling production several years ago with a director who was indecisive, petulant, and anxious—someone who seemed to be in over their head. As a result, the production lacked a coherent, consistent vision; shooting days ran long, nerves ran short, and there was no leadership to help the team get through it. Being on that set in such chaotic conditions felt intensely frustrating for my talented friend; she herself could see a clear way through some of the challenges, but she was not in a position to exercise any authority to change things. So instead she practised radical acceptance, which she called "deep surrender": this was the state she learned to get herself into each morning, as she arrived on set braced for another tumultuous day. She acknowledged and accepted that this situation was a mess—and that, for the time being, this mess was her life. That's Epictetus in action, right there: people are not disturbed by things, but by the view they take of them.

Amanda Knox described her epiphany, her sudden acceptance of the sad and terrible reality that was her life in prison, as "a sadness brimming with energy beneath the surface, because I was alive with myself and my sanity, and the freeing feeling of seeing reality clearly, however sad that reality was … The feeling of clarity … was in realizing that however small, cruel, sad, and unfair this life was, it was *my* life. Mine to make meaning out of, mine to live to the best of my ability. There was no more waiting. There was only now."

Are you waiting for something? Some imagined point in time when everything will be … *better*? If you are living in a state of anticipation for a future that feels more resolved, stable, and under control, the fact is that you're missing out on life right now, uncomfortable and imperfect as it may be. And that is another small grace of a cancer diagnosis: immediacy. There's a sudden clarity about what is happening right now—not just that it is happening, but the enormous value of tuning in to it. For the many months of my cancer treatment in 2009, I felt I saw the world around me as I had never seen it before. The modular sounds of passing strangers' conversations, the taste of a ripe pear, the pattern of light falling on a neighbour's rooftop, fragrance from a spring blossom—countless details leapt out at me, with a significance for which I had never previously given them credit. Random moments in an ordinary day suddenly bloomed with vitality and virtue.

The fact is, each one of us is fragile, but we expend a great deal of effort pushing that reality to the side. Until something happens to remind us: a health scare, a near-miss accident, a great loss, even old age. Research out of the Stanford Center on Longevity finds that older people are happier, on average, than those of younger or middle age. That sense of contentment has been attributed to the shifting of priorities that accompanies a growing sense of impermanence: as we age, or as we face a serious medical challenge, time becomes more precious and the immediate is suddenly enough. An increasingly uncertain future has a surprisingly positive impact on older people, due to a readjusting of perspective.

Austrian psychiatrist and Holocaust survivor Viktor

Frankl created the ultimate testimony to the power of perspective in the face of adversity. In *Man's Search for Meaning*, he recounted many moments of solace and consolation that breathed life and hope into his unspeakably tortured days as a prisoner of the Nazis during the Second World War. He had lost his mother, his father, and his brother in the concentration camps; his view of humanity was forever altered by the cruel treachery of his captors and even some of his fellow captives. But he remained resolute in his own moral goodness, committed to acts of compassion and caring toward needy prisoners. He described a conscious practice of observing the beauty of nature, of noticing and appreciating the hope a glorious sunset can provide in a desolate grey landscape of misery. Our uniqueness as individuals is important, of course, but as Frankl wrote in his collection of lectures *Yes to Life: In Spite of Everything*, there is also uniqueness within every day, every hour, and every moment. And to pause and really see that is to add the weight of a terrible and beautiful responsibility to our lives.

What is it about a dire existential challenge that suddenly imbues the most ordinary of days with a feeling of awe, and otherwise mundane experiences with a sense of enchantment? It must be in no small part because those ordinary days are a reprieve from all the ugly, frightening aspects of otherwise harsh circumstances. The scent of summer rain is a gift after breathing in the smell of hospital disinfectant. Think of the peaceful sound of a quiet neighbourhood at nightfall through an open window, flanked by the distant hum of traffic; the careful devotion the local greengrocer applies to setting out the fruit in tidy rows each morning; the camaraderie of a boisterous pack of teenagers bursting to tell stories over one another on their walk home from school. These gifts are always there. They were there before I got sick with cancer … so why hadn't I noticed them before? Probably because I was too focused on whatever plan I had for the life I was building or working toward, rather than being awake to the life I was in. The threat of that life coming to a premature end made me scramble to soak up all it was offering right now; the uncertainty of what my future held yanked me right back to the present, allowing me to behold its remarkable riches.

The real challenge is trying to retain that clarity when health is restored. When the schedule of hospital visits tapers from daily to weekly, from monthly to biannual. What swoops in, when you're eventually only at the hospital once a year for a check-up, to dull the sense of awe? Plans, hopes, and a forward pitch. We can't help ourselves. If a blessing of poor health is appreciating the grace of small moments, an equally potent blessing of robustness is daring to dream beyond. How—I ask myself now, as I muddle through these ailing, uncomfortable days with undiagnosed health woes, neither fully alive nor fearing imminent death—can we hold onto both at the same time?

Is there a way for us to see each day through that clear-eyed and appreciative lens without having to fall ill or be thrown in jail? There is, after all, a last time for everything. With or without a terminal diagnosis, we all have to say goodbye to parts of our lives; we just usually never know when. We can't tell it's the last time when we're in the middle of it. It's a sentiment that's rooted in ancient Greek philosophy and evoked by Joni Mitchell's famous lyric from "Big Yellow Taxi": we don't know what we have until it's gone. The Stoics practised something called the last time contemplation; by reframing a mundane activity with the possibility that it may never happen again, it becomes imbued with value and a bittersweet appreciation of the moment.

The next time you're stuck in a situation that feels frustrating and not what you wanted, pause for a second to ask yourself how you would feel if you never got to do it again. When I find myself stressed about running late, or angered by a slight, or grouchy about having to clean up someone else's mess, or bored by a droning conversation, or fuming in gridlocked traffic, I try to remind myself of the times I spent in hospitals wondering whether I'd be able to run late for anything or clean up a messy kitchen ever again.

What if something changed your circumstances so that you could no longer drive? You could find yourself missing the chance to sit stuck in a traffic jam, not realizing how fortunate you were to be able to operate a vehicle. Don't dwell on the possibility of terrible things happening to you or your loved ones—that's unproductive anxiety. But do consider, for a moment, the possibility that you may be doing something for the last time.

> Sometimes you're doing really well. Then, after three or four years, everything inexplicably crashes like a house of cards and you have to rebuild it. It's not like you get to a point where you're all right for the rest of your life.
>
> —*Patti Smith*

There are probably more frightening things than learning you have a recurrence of cancer: being held at gunpoint; watching your child dangle precariously from a high place. It's not a competition, but trust me when I tell you that getting cancer *again* is a colossal and terrifying blow.

The second time I was diagnosed with breast cancer (not the way anyone wants to begin a sentence) was far more public than the first. By October 1, 2018, I was the host of Toronto's number-one afternoon radio show; my voice, my name, my irreverent sense of humour, and a whole lot else about me were woven into the fabric of people's daily lives. Radio is the most intimate of mediums; when you sit in your car grinding through a tough commute, or wipe your eyes chopping onions in the kitchen during dinner prep, your afternoon radio host is right there with you. I talk, you listen, we commune.

This was years after my initial breast cancer—like almost-a-decade-and-I-wear-nail-polish-again-and-don't-think-about-cancer-much-anymore later. Aside from annual check-ins with my oncology team, breast cancer was squarely in my rear-view mirror. My oldest son, Reggie, had started university, on a scholarship to a music school in Boston; Harper and Miles were moving through adolescence and navigating high school. One late August weekend, we were all together at a cousin's cottage. When the time came for Sunday morning's round-the-island swim, I was in. The last-half-of-summer sun shone in between cloud clusters as I donned my bathing suit and psyched myself up for this annual tradition. Then suddenly, as we stood bracing ourselves for the plunge into the chilly, late-summer waters, something shifted. Clouds moved in and the wind picked up, bringing the full force of the Georgian Bay waves crashing through my plan of swimming breaststroke for such a long distance.

To avoid gulping mouthfuls, I swam front crawl instead—an unusual choice for me. The route went clockwise around the island, so I pulled harder with my left arm to stay on course. I finished last (no surprise there) but no one cared, not even me. By nightfall, on the trip back to the city, my left underarm hurt. There was a pull under there, as though the muscle was catching on a latch. Something tugging.

"I think I pulled a muscle on that swim," I said. "My left arm really hurts."

"You swam hard today. You probably woke up a few muscles you forgot you had." Grant was probably right. Right?

I called my doctor the following day. By the time I was in her office it had been forty-eight hours since my swim and the pain was gone. "I guess it was a pulled muscle," I said.

My doctor checked and confirmed that there was nothing there. "I don't feel anything," she said. But she's the thorough type so, given my history on the left side, she ordered an ultrasound. Just to be safe.

Unclear ultrasound images led to more tests, an MRI, and a visit with the surgeon—the same surgeon who had cut off my left breast nearly ten years previously. Hello again. He checked under my armpit, said he too found nothing suspect. "I can't feel anything there," this top breast cancer surgeon said.

Hallelujah and amen. Worry warriors, stand down.

But, he told me as I tucked in my shirt and prepared to skip home, he'd like to order a biopsy. *Just to be safe.*

The biopsy showed malignancy; the tumour would need to be removed. Pronto. As would the entire network of lymph nodes under my left arm. Another misshapen feature of my torso, another meandering scar, another assault on the pretence that all was or could ever be well in my world.

Hadn't I already learned my lesson? Surrendered to the impossibility and futility of control, appreciated the small wonders of my precious given days? *I already did this! I* get *it, for fuck's sake.*

"Illness frightens us because it's chaotic," Emily St. John Mandel writes in her novel *Sea of Tranquility*. "There's an awful randomness about it." A sense of randomness may seem misplaced in the case of recurrence, and yet it's not. To be fully present for the recovery from illness number one, to lean into life with an enhanced appreciation for its beautiful fragility, the survivor doesn't spend time dwelling on the possibility of illness number two.

Memento mori. The whispered reminder that you will die rings a little louder upon emerging from the dark tunnel of cancer treatment, and that awareness plunges the cancer survivor—or at least this cancer survivor—into the fullness of life, having tasted the bitter threat of its imminent end. The alternative is to dwell on the fear of recurrence, which is both upsetting and life-limiting; we can easily be so anxious about whether an illness might recur that we hold ourselves back from fully taking part in the very life we are afraid of losing.

I had celebrated my recovered health. For close to a decade, I had held it in a strong embrace, enough that I came to believe that my cancer had been—as so many are—an anomaly. The tumour fully excised, the surrounding tissue radiated to an arid tract of spiritless flesh, any possible lurking cancer cells choked and starved of fuel by a daily dose of medication … I was in the clear.

So why did my cancer come back? To this day, not one of the specialists in my team of care has an answer to that mystery. Was it even a recurrence? Or was it a new primary cancer? I never knew which of those options to hope for.

The unpredictability of illness is what frightens us: the fickleness of its strike, the unknowable nature of its impact. How much will it hurt? How long will it last? Will it come back? Is this one going to be the one that kills me? Serious illness is hard enough to go through once; the victorious relief when the treatments end is hard-earned. Having to repeat the trip is downright defeating. Unless it isn't.

Illness is, as Susan Sontag called it, "the night-side of life, a more onerous citizenship." And that is the hard-won and difficult truth of a second terrifying diagnosis. Illness, complete with all its uncertainties, *is* life. At the time, I saw my first cancer as a life lesson, a one-off mystery that I survived, a brief divergence from the path I had envisioned for my life. Its recurrence was a reminder that these health crises were not detours on the journey; they *were* the journey. The path I had imagined for myself crumbled over a steep edge. Recurrence, health, the random chaos of everything in between—this was happening. There was no dress rehearsal. This was my life.

The Stoics argued that the way to deal with adversity is not simply to accept it, but to come to love it. By the time there is a diagnosis, a conviction, a loss of whatever kind, resistance is futile. The unforeseen blow has been struck. The Stoic approach is *amor fati*, which translates from the Latin as a "love of one's fate."

In his own writing about the concept of *amor fati*, German philosopher Friedrich Nietzsche described the mindset as "not to wish for anything other than that which is; whether behind, ahead, or for all eternity. Not just to put up with the inevitable—much less to hide it from oneself, for all idealism is lying to oneself in the face of the necessary—but to love it."

Loving a cancer diagnosis sounds far-fetched, but given that the alternative is stubborn resistance, it's a worthy goal. It's an extension of the *wabi-sabi* attitude I have chosen to take toward my body—savaged and rearranged by multiple surgeries, patterned with scars. *Wabi-sabi* is a Japanese aesthetic that celebrates imperfection and impermanence, rooted in an appreciation of transience: a belief that brokenness is beautiful, since nothing lasts and nothing is ever perfect. But accepting hardship is not to be confused with giving up—quite the opposite. Accepting and embracing the difficulties we face allows us to get on with making the best of whatever is happening and the time we have. The challenges we've been dealt become like oxygen, fuelling the fire of our lives.

"How do I make that life worth living?" Amanda Knox asked herself in the midst of her epiphany of sadness, as she realized that her wrongful conviction was not a temporary departure from the life she was meant to lead—but was, in fact, her life. In the face of overwhelming adversity and chronic uncertainty, the big questions of how to be and how to feel can be paralyzing. For Knox, answers came more easily when the question got smaller: "How can I make my life worth living *today*?" That's a question we can all ask, and answer, repeatedly. Knox found agency and serenity in simple activities within the prison walls. "Doing sit ups, walking laps, writing a letter, reading a book—these things were enough to make a day worth living. I didn't know if they were enough to make a life worth living, but I remained open and curious to the possibility."

If I factor in a minor surgery to remove melanoma from my left leg—yes, a third diagnosis—it's easy to characterize my life as one plagued by cancer; easy to imagine that more illness and despair are my fate. It's also a short trip from there to feeling robbed of overall health, of various body parts, of a more carefree life. I could, quite legitimately, get caught up in the sadness of that loss. When we experience an avalanche of unforeseen change, we can wind up so busy clinging to the way it used to be and grieving what we have lost that we aren't able to get a grip on what we have right now or reach for what could be. Or be open to what is yet to come.

As I struggle to manage a mysterious and long-term debilitating condition, it's easy to think that perhaps I am a sickly person destined to be unwell forever—that the toll of life on my body is proving too much for it to take. That my dreams of a long and active life with the people I love are a naive fantasy. But that mindset doesn't help much. It would also be a situation akin to what James Joyce described in his short story "A Painful Case" as "Mister Duffy lived a short distance from his body." When our minds race ahead of ourselves, we are not fully present for what is happening. To treat life, as Somerset Maugham cautioned, as a pilgrimage to some future and better existence "is to disown its present value."

If I pay closer attention to the life I do have, those feelings of fear and foreboding fall away. When I stop to look around me, I notice the delicate pale lashes of my toffee-coloured mutt Hugo, and hear the breathy sneezes he breaks into when he sees his leash come out and gets deliriously excited for a walk. I notice how no two sets of tree branches have the exact same structure. I feel the weight of my feet on the ground as I stride through the imperfect life that I get to be here for today. If I shift from taking these things for granted to paying close attention to their every detail, savouring how much meaning and comfort they add to any given moment in my day, I feel them more deeply. And at the same time my mind is so locked into whatever is happening right here and now that there's no room for anxiety about what may be yet to come.

This isn't a Jedi mind trick—though I suppose in a way it is, because it works to dispel anxiety about what could have been or what may be. *Fear is the path to the dark side.* In any case, it's not deceptive, not a shiny object or a nullifying warping of reality to distract from the truth. The wisdom of living and thinking this way is that it is in fact the truth. We humans are awfully good at convincing ourselves that our forecast of worst-case scenarios is reality, when really the future in which those possibilities will unfold hasn't taken place yet—so who the hell knows? The "what if" engine that drives our jitters crashes to a halt when we hunker down in the exact moment of where we are and what is currently true. We tend to assume we know what *will* be true, and we don't like to be wrong. We are trained to calculate and predict outcomes, based on the available evidence. I have had three cancer diagnoses. How is that not a basis for trepidation for my future? But while we must hold within us the chapters from our past, rich with experience and teaching as they are, we must also—as the Jedi warrior reassures us—*carry them lightly*.

The chambered nautilus is a cephalopod—a sea creature whose eyes sit almost immediately atop its limbs. You'd recognize it by the cross-section view of its shell: a golden spiral containing multiple separate cavities. Over its lifespan the nautilus builds more, and increasingly larger, chambers of shell. Though it only ever resides within the most recently grown portion, it carries the increasingly large collection of empty chambers around on its back. This is an evolutionary feature that at first glance looks like a great hindrance to mobility for the humble mollusc—kind of like having to pay rent on every apartment you've ever lived in, even after you move out. But the truth is that while the bulky shell may appear a cumbersome burden, it is what ensures the creature is buoyant. By adjusting the volume and density of water within its hollow cavities, the chambered nautilus can control its dives and ascents—making use of where it has been and what it has lived through as a means to stay afloat and navigate the waters of the present. It's a beautiful metaphor for how to live through hardship: stay present and live in the moment, while lightly carrying your memories and accrued wisdom as a tool for navigation.

The American physician, poet, and polymath Oliver Wendell Holmes Sr. wrote a poetic tribute to the endangered mollusc in his 1858 poem "The Chambered Nautilus":

> Year after year beheld the silent toil
> That spread his lustrous coil;
> Still, as the spiral grew,
> He left the past year's dwelling for the new,
>
> . . .
>
> Built up its idle door,
> Stretched in his last-found home,
>   and knew the old no more.

Isn't that an ideal strategy for how to roll with the punches? Remember what we have been through, appreciate whatever strength and resilience those challenges taught us, and be held buoyant by them, not weighed down. Take each day as it comes, control what we can, and surrender to the rest. Decide, as the Stoic philosophers suggest, what meaning can be extracted from even the most arduous of circumstances.

Applying the principle of entropy—or randomness—to these overwhelming, change-filled days we are muddling through is somehow liberating and reassuring. A call to humility in the face of uncertainty. Of course things feel chaotic; all systems will eventually devolve from order into chaos. There is only one possible permutation in which each piece of a puzzle is in the right place and the image is complete, and an infinite number in which the pieces are jumbled, out of order. We keep trying to hold the disarray in check and assemble the puzzle pieces into a satisfying image; it is our life's purpose. Yet somehow we must also leave space for the certainty that any success is destined to be short-lived. *Pro tempore.* Everything, ultimately, is *pro tempore*, whether we like it or not.

Uncertainty, syn.: *Ambivalence*

Floating blissfully in a silky cloud of dim awareness, I slowly emerge from my afternoon nap. I wish it would last, that delicious, delirious, semi-conscious state. But of course, it cannot, which is exactly what makes it so precious. The birds calling outside my window, the traffic sounds from the street below—they bring me back to the world, and soon enough I am fully awake. This is what my days are made of: simple, restful, low-energy undertakings that pass for activity. I nap; I watch TV shows in the bathtub; I read on the couch; I make simple meals; I take short walks around the neighbourhood with the dog; I go to bed early.

An afternoon nap or Netflix in a bubble bath—that was the stuff of dreamy fantasy for the busy working person I used to be. Now it's something I rely on to function. A leisurely walk and a good book on the couch are luxuries, to be sure. Most of the time I am mindful of how fortunate I am to be able to experience this long-term health uncertainty in this way. But some days the whole picture brings me down; I think because it is making me feel old. Is this how I'm going to want to live for the rest of my life? Satisfied with little things, leaving the striving and dynamism to the next generation and their round-the-clock energies.

But maybe I'm conflating two things that are happening at the same time.

I am a woman in her late fifties, watching her body change. Each day I bid a slow, inexorable farewell to my old hair and skin and youth in the mirror.

That would be happening anyway, I remind myself.

But those feelings of loss are intensified by the lacklustre way in which I spend most days. My former body, its ability to leap and stride into action, its nimble pivots in the dance of a full life—those are cloudy memories now.

What does my future hold? How much more of my active youthful way of being will have deteriorated by the time I get better? What will feeling better even look like? Maybe everything I treasured about living a full life is gone—

But I'm getting ahead of myself. Recognizing the train of anxious thinking picking up speed, I visualize a railroad switch that will divert it onto a different track, shifting its direction toward another mental destination. The worry train is a high-speed bullet to nowhere good. So I stop. I come back to sit, right here.

Today is all I have, right now, this immediate moment. This footfall on a slow walk. What else can I pay attention to? A dog barks nearby. Yesterday's rain puddles are drying slowly on the warm pavement. A neighbour works intently in his garden, his gloved fingers muddy as he cultivates what lies before him.

ANSWERS AND QUESTIONS

Have patience with everything that remains unsolved in your heart … live in the question.

—*Rainer Maria Rilke,* Letters to a Young Poet

IT IS A MILD DAY in late June when the protracted hurly-burly of medical investigations and examinations comes to a halt. The eight-and-a-half-month-long carnival of bright lights and beeping, whirring machines, pricey parking lots and long pale hallways and elevator rides up and down in nearly every one of the city's hospitals, the panoply of new faces, my story of ailments repeated like a broken record, an enervating spree of waiting and wondering—it suddenly ends, like the power has gone out at the fairground and the Ferris wheel slows to a stop.

It ends down another long hallway, at an appointment with another specialist, another new face. Blondish wavy hair, kind eyes, gentle energy. This one—I check her name tag—is with the departments of internal medicine and endocrinology. Haven't I already seen each of those? My heart begins to sink. Another futile effort; another well-intentioned expert with no answers who will refer me to yet another well-intentioned expert with no answers. But as I run through my story this time, cataloguing the confounding discomforts, bracing for yet another mystified response, I can tell something is different. The doctor nods with understanding, doesn't take notes. When she speaks at last it's in a firm tone, her voice ringing with confidence and certainty. "Ohh," she says with a sympathetic tilt of her head, "that's definitely long COVID."

I am so startled to have an answer, it takes me a minute to appreciate the relief of hearing it.

Wait, what . . . ? Really? You're sure?

"Absolutely. That deep sinus pressure and post-nasal discomfort you're describing, I've heard that from a lot of patients in our long COVID clinic."

I have been sent to this office after finally establishing, through a certain blood test that can distinguish natural COVID antibodies from those created by the vaccine, that I did at some point, without ever knowing it or testing positive, have COVID. I never blew my nose, never coughed or lost my sense of taste, but I had it, alright. Although the nucleocapsid test could not identify when I had been infected, it was sufficient evidence for my doctor to refer me to a long COVID clinic for an assessment. As I describe the litany of other symptoms that accompany the sinus aches, this long COVID specialist nods in recognition. "Yup," she says, "this all fits."

I have the urge to stand up and give her a hug. But why?

There is no cure for this extended malaise, and not much in the way of medical understanding of its path. Much of the anecdotal evidence of long COVID sufferers involves years of unpredictability and seemingly chronic debilitation. And yet, here in the dimly lit office of this wise, empathetic expert, having an answer at last feels like a gift.

What part of my life do I get back? Not my energy, not my ability to walk quickly or run up a flight of stairs, not peaceful silence in my ears or uninterrupted sleep. No, all I get from this diagnosis is the ability to know why I feel this way. The certainty of a name, the clarity of a condition that is itself a guarantee of further uncertainty. The opportunity to sit squarely in that uncertainty, call it what it is and accept it. This is my life. The peculiar salmagundi of symptoms that has been my ongoing malaise makes sense for the first time in nearly a year: I am a COVID long-hauler. Puzzle pieces swirl before my eyes and click gently into place. But of course, the image that forms is one of more discomfort, more restrictions, more weariness and hardship. The question that emerges is: *How do I live my life within these radically limited bounds?* It is the reckoning of every person who knows suffering, the task of anyone who faces the uncertainty of an unclear future. And it is most definitely the reality of every patient coping with long COVID, a newly emerging condition that no one really understands.

What should I do? I ask this sympathetic doctor. She knows enough to identify the problem; my first instinct is to cling to her as a lifeline for how to solve it. Blessed with a single piece of certainty, I feel the immediate hunger for more. The familiar urge to rush through the uncertainty and make this discomfort go away. The implication in my question being: How do I get back the health and comfort I used to feel? How can I turn myself back into the able-bodied and clear-headed woman I used to be? When can I function the way I should be able to in this world? What do I have to do to make this problem disappear?

"This is an opportunity to increase your tolerance for hard things," she tells me. "We all have an impulse to reject the parts of us that are weak, to resist when we don't feel well. We struggle against things we don't like. But we're just in an argument with reality. Can you make friends with your long COVID? Can you learn to love it?"

Long COVID was the thing I feared most through the pandemic. I had heard anecdotal reports of lasting COVID cases, of otherwise active people being reduced to limp piles of achy fatigue. And so I washed my hands with dedication, wore a mask, and got all my vaccines. How did this happen? How can I possibly learn to love the predator I most dreaded?

The impulse to be angered by the idea of befriending my enemy is surprisingly short-lived. It is one of the hardest things I have been asked to do, and yet a part of me understands almost immediately that it is, of course, the sole option. *Amor fati.*

This is happening. No amount of wishing it otherwise, or wishing it over, can change that reality. Which leaves radical acceptance as the only available choice. I know now what *this* is—and that is valuable information. The doctors have ruled out a long list of other frightening possibilities, and for that I can be glad. Long COVID is not a terminal illness. I am grateful for that too.

When we name something for what it is, we can quantify its power. The beast has emerged from the shadows, and now—instead of cowering with fear of what it might be—I can see its size and shape and choose how to respond to its presence.

"You will get better. I can't tell you how long it will take. Some of my patients have taken up to two years. But I can tell you that you'll get there. In the meantime, eat an anti-inflammatory diet, keep taking your vitamins, and meditate every day. But the best thing you can do for your recovery is to work on being okay with the discomfort and not to fight it."

Diagnosis: post-acute sequelae of COVID-19.

I have a chronic illness with no definitive endpoint.

Prescription: sit with the uncertainty of what happens next.

"The power of belief is the whole game." That is the mantra, and the basis of her groundbreaking psychological research, of Ellen Langer. For decades, work in Langer's lab at Harvard has focused on the mind-body continuum, on the utter folly of considering the two as separate entities, and on the degree to which our mindset impacts our performance and our outcome. Her work on the influence of mindset is widely regarded, and required reading in a great many introductory psychology courses. It is even cited in an episode of *The Simpsons*.

What is a mindset? An attitude, a choice of which thoughts to make habitual, a conscious decision about which neural pathways to exercise—which wolf to feed, as it were.

In her 2007 "chambermaid study," Langer and her colleagues gathered health data from a group of chambermaids—eighty-four women working in a range of different locations. Too tired at the end of their days spent cleaning hotel suites to ever get to the gym for exercise, the participants' weights and rates of diabetes were, at the outset of the study, a reflection of poor fitness. One half of the group was instructed to rethink their hardworking days—pushing trolleys, lifting heavy trays, lunging to strip bed linens—as good exercise, an effort that would satisfy the surgeon general's recommendations for an active lifestyle. In their minds, they didn't need the gym because they were already exercising. The control group was not given that instruction. After four weeks, the group that identified their labour as an actual workout showed decreases in weight, blood pressure, body fat, waist-to-hip ratio, and body mass index, compared to the control group. All because of what stories they told themselves about what they were doing.

What stories are we telling ourselves?

The chambermaid study is one of many—from Langer's lab and elsewhere—that illustrate the impact of mindset on outcome. Langer argues that our degree of anxiety and unease correlates directly with the degree to which we are checked out of the present moment and what is happening in front of us. Like the Stoic philosophers and Eastern mindfulness practitioners before her, Langer maintains that it is our minds racing ahead of the present moment and imagining what yet may come—or ruminating on what has already passed—that generates worry and stress. Her research shows that even from a Western, evidence-based standpoint, paying more attention to the present moment can generate wellness.

No worry before its time.

We need, Langer maintains after her decades of research studying the mindless automaticity of so much human behaviour, to stop confusing the stability of our mindset with the stability of the underlying phenomenon. Assuming, predicting, and believing something is not in fact evidence of that something's existence. Langer's research studies seem to show clear proof of the need to stop ourselves getting caught up in runaway thoughts that aren't helpful, and to recognize all that we don't know for sure. We should, she argues, *increase* our uncertainty.

Viewed that way, there is a hopefulness that emerges from not knowing what is coming next. If the future is not within our control, then it only stands to reason that anything is possible; within the wide-open spectrum of uncertainty, there is room for opportunity and influence.

Anyone who claims to be able to predict outcomes is only relying on what has come before and extrapolating from the data. Science tracks probabilities, some of which we mistake for absolutes. We put so much faith into algorithms, weather-tracking systems, economic forecasting models, and well-paid analysts and pundits, and yet educated guesses are all these prognostications really are. There are always other variables in the mix—human ingenuity, compassion, evolutionary survival instincts—many of which are unknowable and immeasurable. As such, we cannot possibly know for certain what the future holds. What we *can* know and control is our mindset. And our degree of hope.

In the face of the stupefying exponential change brought on by AI technology that threatens our role on the earth, dire climate forecasts that put our very existence into question, and every other unknowable aspect of our high-octane age of emergency, the idea of staying hopeful can feel like an insult to our intelligence.

But let's take a beat to distinguish between hope and toxic positivity. The latter kind of cheer is a mindless reflex; a disconnection from a deeper fear of how out of control one feels, cheaply masked with saccharine bromides. Toxic positivity is at best trite and at worst inauthentic. We cannot "you got this!" our way through the torrents of change confronting us every day. Hope is something altogether different. Hope is fuel for growth; a mindset of possibility. And no social shift has ever happened without it. To achieve a better world, we must first imagine it.

In a research paper entitled "The Black Radical Imagination: A Space of Hope and Possible Futures," published in the journal *Frontiers in Neurology*, American neuropsychologist Tanisha G. Hill-Jarrett explains the critical role of hope and imagination in the neural networks of the subjects in her study and how that connects to societal change more broadly. Black Americans have roughly double the risk of developing Alzheimer's disease and related dementias. Hill-Jarrett's research shows a clear connection between hopeful imagining and neuroplasticity—the brain's ability to forge new neural pathways.

"A cognitive neuroscience perspective," she writes, "considers imagination to be the representational engagement with that which is absent." Believing in the possibility of progress toward a future we want but cannot yet see—only in the mind's eye. Tracking brain patterns of elderly Black Americans employing "radical hope"—defined in her paper as the ability to imagine the world, life, and social institutions not as they are but as they might otherwise be—Hill-Jarrett observed a clear connection between hope and successful outcomes in those subjects who were able to modify the structural organization of their brains through the act of radically reimagining an equitable society. "The radical imagination brings possible futures 'back' to work on the present, to inspire action."

In the context of seniors' well-being, imagining a better future can have positive effects on brain health. People who feel more hopeful have a larger and better-developed part of the brain known as the supplementary motor area—responsible for planning voluntary movements and critical for turning cognition into action. But Hill-Jarrett points out the more far-reaching impact of hope and a radical imagination, beyond individual brain health. "It is the collective imagination—a group process through which knowledge and new ideas are co-produced—that undergirds many social justice movements toward Black collective liberation."

There is no way forward through the massive challenges that face our world—from climate to equity to social justice to peace—without hope. It is emotionally and practically essential. American writer and civil rights activist James Baldwin knew it, when he famously said despair was not an emotion he could afford. We cannot, he reasoned, tell our children there is no hope.

Again, hope is quite distinct from optimism. An optimistic outlook is more passive than a hopeful one. That supplementary motor area of the hopeful brain fills us with bright purpose and allows us to act, which is of course essential for change. In her book *Hope in the Dark*, essayist Rebecca Solnit points out that taking some sort of purposeful step is the key ingredient of hope. Optimists and pessimists each cling to their own certainties, which excuse them from taking action. Hope is something different. Hope embraces the unknown.

So where do we find hope amid the darkness? Look for the people, the stories, the experiences, and the actionables that lean into progress. Protect and celebrate something in nature that buoys your spirit—awe walk, anyone? It gets easier to find the more we look for it: think of the "sorting for red" exercise, and try only sorting for evidence of growth, for acts of kindness and humanity, for innovation and research. In his award-winning book *How to Be a Climate Optimist: Blueprints for a Better World*, Chris Turner offers up a bounty of evidence for hope to offset our climate angst, and reminds us how unhelpful doom-thinking is. His decades of research—travelling to cities and countries with a deep commitment to sustainability; speaking with architects and touring off-grid facilities that herald a brighter future—give the reader so much hope to work with, as they catalogue the rapid pace of real and sustainable change that is already well underway around the world. I notice how much better I feel every time I read that book.

Surrounding ourselves with acts of radical imagination, becoming part of something constructive, shifts the brain to a set of neural pathways that invigorate.

And yet …

Hope can also have a distracting allure. It feels somehow counter to the wisdom of surrendering to the present moment, however uncomfortable it may be. American Buddhist nun Pema Chödrön cautions against the siren call of hope, arguing it can be an addictive escape from the discomfort of life's fundamental mysteries—of what lies outside our control. Suffering, Chödrön writes in her book *When Things Fall Apart*, starts to dissolve when we let go of the hope of hiding or escaping from it. Radical acceptance, here we are again.

But if we clearly cannot evolve and thrive without hope, the question I find myself coming back to is this: Where is the balance between hope for the future and acceptance of the present?

One possible answer comes from the Harvard Business School, of all places. On the school's website I stumbled upon an essay about survival psychology, written for business leaders struggling to manage operations at the onset of the pandemic. The advice was to adopt something called the Stockdale Paradox. Admiral James Stockdale was an officer during the Vietnam War. When his plane was shot down over enemy territory, he was captured, tortured, and held hostage for over seven years. Having watched many of his fellow prisoners give up and die during the excruciating ordeal, Stockdale attributed his survival to his ability to hold firmly to the faith that he would make it out. But he was quick to distinguish his approach from optimism. "You must never confuse faith that you will prevail in the end—which you can never afford to lose—with the discipline to confront the most brutal facts of your current reality." There needs to be a balance of hope and realism, which can feel like conflicting feelings to hold at the same time—that's the paradox.

Stockdale never lost faith that his own story would end with his release—and what's more, he held firm to his conviction that he would not just prevail over his suffering but go on to make it the defining event of his life: one he would, in retrospect, not trade for anything.

That is some serious tenacity—and an echo of Epictetus. We get to decide what we do with the hard things that happen to us. And that doesn't just apply to CEOs trying to manage productivity during a crisis. All harrowing challenges with uncertain and unknowable outcomes must be faced head-on, and endured with hopeful determination.

What does it look like to stay grounded in sober reality and yet remain hopeful about the possibilities? We can take mindful, forward-looking steps as acts of compassion—for ourselves and those around us. Hopeful thoughts and actions are a gift to our present and future world, evidence of our capacity for grace. And yet that tenderness must be offered without expectation, allowed to coexist with uncertainty; it cannot be a delusion, or seen as a gateway to happiness. There is no antidote for uncertainty, not even hope.

~

Can you make friends with your long COVID? The doctor's question could also be asked this way: *How comfortable are you with taking a compassionate, mindful attitude to the reality that lies before you?*

I ponder the lessons baked into her query. She was, effectively, instructing me to find a calm, hopeful way forward through my condition. To make friends with the enemy.

As I dissect the basic elements of friendship, what can I find here in my illness?

So far, joy and laughter are not part of the long COVID package. But friendship also has at its core a sense of appreciation, even admiration. I respect each one of my friends for the many beautiful and valuable qualities they bring to my life. That seems a more promising route to a take when it comes to my lingering post-viral companion. Is there anything about it that I can perhaps not admire, but appreciate? What are its best qualities?

Undercutting the ability to function as I once did; slowing me down with great discomfort; undoing whatever hold I thought I had over my day; idealizing the way things used to be in the past; throwing future possibilities and opportunities into question—those are long COVID's worst qualities. Could they also be its best?

For all its vexing impediments to my well-being, my illness is, by that measure, also somewhat instructive. An echo of other, more universally felt challenges. Discomfort, a lack of control—isn't that what every change and uncertain threat brings about? AI, climate peril, political upheaval, viral outbreaks, economic restructuring, global conflicts—all of it, the entire crushing load of chaos coming at us every day, matches the perplexity profile of long COVID.

I can't claim to have achieved equanimity about how unhinged the world has become, but as I figure out how to navigate my personal health crisis it is clear that some of the lessons I'm learning, some of the offerings of this so-called friendship, apply more broadly.

A caring friend fills me with hopeful motivation to investigate, educate, take action where possible.

I find a physiotherapy clinic online that specializes in long COVID rehabilitation. Wary of false promises in the treatment of an emerging condition whose signature is so varied and so little understood, I give it a cautious try. In virtual appointments with a friendly clinician, I learn to measure my energetic output more precisely so as not to overexert myself. I begin to see a trend in the kinds of behaviours that trigger symptoms—rushing to do things quickly, the social pressure to perform, pushing through to do just one more thing before taking time to rest … and I start to deprogram those instincts.

An encouraging friend offers the reminder to observe, be curious, open to possibilities.

As I progress slowly—oh so agonizingly and tediously slowly—back toward a full range of abilities, I am learning to turn much of my old thinking on its head. Barrelling forward is a foolish pace. Our culture of urgency—constant texts and news alerts, notifications and other demands keeping our brains in fight-or-flight mode—is not sustainable. Fight-or-flight is the sympathetic nervous system on high alert; rest-and-digest is its opposite, parasympathetic state. But there is a third option: to be mindfully attuned to what is happening and how it feels. To sit with it.

A compassionate friend says: Take care of yourself. Pause more, slow the fuck down.

It occurs to me that smokers have a built-in reprieve attached to their habit: a smoker's routine is to step away from the bustle and blare of whatever is going on so they can get a nicotine fix. What they also get is a few minutes alone, in the fresh air, with no agenda but to inhale deeply. Why shouldn't non-smokers build that into our days too? So, I do.

Once or twice a day I excuse myself from the world. *Just taking a smoke break.* I sit or recline in a quiet space, close my eyes, and inhale. I feel the bottoms of my feet brushing up against my socks; I feel the life force in my legs, arms, chest, head. I feel the cool whisper of my breath as it passes by the tip of my nose on the way in. Exhaling, I press pause on the pandemonium of moving forward and let go of any agenda. Some problems resolve themselves if we let them.

Allowing a little stillness, taking some time to reflect, opens up opportunities for new growth.

A good friend helps you know yourself more intimately. Feel your fear, identify it, let it pass.

Every so often I read an opinion essay or some other reportage profiling a COVID long-hauler. A formerly active, otherwise healthy professional who now cannot get off the couch; a marathon-running man who hasn't been able to exercise in two years; a once social and lively woman who has to work from home to manage the crippling body aches, tinnitus, and fatigue that have plagued her for nearly four years.

Four. Years.

People send me these articles by way of encouragement, thinking I'll enjoy the company of the shared misery, or as a reminder that medical research continues to seek answers. More often, reading these stories makes me sad. The details are heartbreakingly familiar, the depressing narratives echo my own. I feel my blood flow slow to a gelatinous crawl. Discouraged that this will be a lifelong curse, that my free-wheeling days are over and I'll never live another day without feeling like crap. *Nearly four years.* I recognize my fear kicking in. I know its signature. I sit and let its reverberations rattle through me: a hot flush, a sickening congested feeling in my limbs, my heart elbowing against my ribs in an explosive staccato. By deconstructing its every move, the fear becomes less my own, more of a visitor—like a noxious house guest passing through town. I help her pack up her things and leave.

A wise friend shows me how to exercise patience and humility.

Long COVID is only long in name, of course; the condition has been around for just a few years. Which is a cruelly lengthy sentence for a patient not feeling well, but a very short period in which to gather data and develop a scientific understanding of the problem and how to solve it. Even the medical community is living with a great deal of uncertainty and overwhelm, as more and more people complain of their own confusing jumble of symptoms. There are roughly two hundred different impacts of long COVID, and currently no single test that connects them to a cause. That analytic uncertainty is a challenge for doctors who are accustomed, even reliant, on diagnostic tests to determine what's going on. This period of unknowing will no doubt lead to understanding. But that's small comfort for those who are suffering today. In the meantime, doctors and their patients struggle to make sense of symptoms and navigate a path through the not-yet-known.

All of life is not-yet-known. Except for this bit, right now. This is happening. Every moment gives us an experience of life. I mustn't waste the moments that feel unpleasant and unnerving—it's not as though they count any less in the final tally of a life lived. William James said, "Our life experience will equal what we have paid attention to whether by choice or by default." This is life at the moment, a tempest of uncertainty.

Can you make friends with long COVID? I continue to wrestle with the doctor's question like a riddle. It feels like a Jedi warrior's confounding calling, like Yoda's unthinkable challenge: *Train yourself to let go of everything you fear to lose.* I don't know how to do that, but I do trust in the process of learning.

What I do know how to do by this point is to lean into not having the answers, and to sit in that mystery with comfort and curiosity. I don't know why one bird makes a different sound to another, why no two tree branches take exactly the same shape. I don't have to know where the story goes from here. True confidence is living with uncertainty, whatever shape it takes, and moving forward into possibility.

EPILOGUE

TO BOOKEND WHERE WE BEGAN, I must tell you this: in March 2024, I got well again.

Yes indeed, let me shout it from the rooftops, I am joyfully, energetically, enthusiastically, confidently, and completely better. Back to the dynamic and vibrant self I thought I had lost.

A full explanation of all the recovery involved would in some ways fill another book. But the broad strokes are worth mentioning here, not just to fill out the happy ending but because I think you'll recognize them. Everything I read and learned and shared here in this book about embracing uncertainty came to bear on my recovery.

I faced the hard truths of long COVID's myriad symptoms and how little the condition is understood.

I felt the sensations of fear and sorrow as they flared, but resolved not to be undone by them—and I let them pass.

I remained determined to recover, and held—however tenuously at times—to the belief I would get through.

I remained open to learning about new possibilities for improvement.

I stayed proactive, researching and asking questions. This led me to stumble upon emerging evidence for a neuroplastic approach to treating chronic illness, based on multiple recommendations of how it had worked to treat long COVID.

I kept an open mind to the possibility of a positive outcome, embracing something I had not considered before and was not at all certain I understood.

I learned how to harness the power of the mind to influence outcomes in the body. This involved using principles of cognitive behavioural therapy to interrupt unintentional and unconscious neural patterns of fear and anxiety around my ongoing symptoms, and applying the principles of neuroplasticity to create new, more helpful neural pathways.

I chose carefully what I paid attention to, began to focus less on the aches and pains of my condition; I resisted any rush to a panic that might imbue symptoms with catastrophic meaning.

I learned to trust in my body's history of healing and recovery, and to remind myself of my strength and resilience.

I took (and take) a lot of awe walks, restoring my spirits with gratitude for all there is to behold right here in the present moment.

I understand how little control I have over what happens next, how precious this whole wild ride is, how much there is to wonder at—all we don't fully understand about our bodies, our minds, and the world that beckons us each morning. How much strength there is in that uncertainty; its power to make everything more meaningful.

This is not how the story ends, because my story continues. So does yours. Through turbulent geopolitical bargaining, perilous economic upheaval, burning cities, social reckoning, and all manner of unknowables.

My hope is that this chapter in my story may be of comfort, wherever it finds you in yours.

Onward.

ACKNOWLEDGEMENTS

EVERY CREATIVE UNDERTAKING IS itself a foray into the unknown. I am endlessly grateful to have had so much support through this one.

Thank you to Deb Farquharson for loyal and loving camaraderie in the curiosity.

To Marina Dempster for thoughts on finding courage amidst the fear.

To Jonathan Blake for the enthusiasm and the physics lesson.

To Patti Brennan for such magnificent company, always, and for being a wise and encouraging first reader.

To Anne Fenn for creative companionship.

Thank you to Cindy Ryley for the wide-open verandah on which to write every summer and the lifelong friendship that comes with it.

Thank you to Emmy Laybourne, a constant spark.

To Ed Manning, Michael Goldfried, and Lisa

Papademetriou, the most creative, funny, and supportive writing group ever.

Thank you to my editor Shivaun Hearne, who saw right from the jump exactly what I wanted this book to be and whose sharp eye and steady hand helped me get it there.

To Jenny McWha, Gemma Wain, and the rest of the terrific team at House of Anansi, for putting so much care and attention into these pages and making this book the strongest it could be.

To Melissa Shirley, Emma Rhodes, Jessey Glibbery, Emma Davis, and their teams for sharing it so enthusiastically with the world.

And the OGs:

To my literary agent Samantha Haywood, always masterful at seeing possibility in uncertainty. Sam's ready smile and unflappable faith in this project helped me find my way through the thicket. Thank you for championing the idea, the writing, and the writer.

To my three boys, Reggie, Harper, and Miles Gordon, whose artistic passions are a true joy to behold. Thank you for being forever playful and brave, and for the rock-steady faith in your mama.

And to Grant, terra firma under all the uncertainty. Thank you for the love affair every single day.

NOTES

Prologue

Writing, as the poet Louise Glück said: Alice Winkler (host), *What It Takes*, podcast, episode 55, "Louise Glück: Revenge Against Circumstance," American Academy of Achievement, July 31, 2017, achievement.org/video/louise-gluck/.

A. R. Ammons put it succinctly: A. R. Ammons, "Old Geezer," in *Brink Road* (Norton, 1996). Used by permission of W. W. Norton & Company Inc.

Big Uncertain World

As American poet laureate Joy Harjo suggests: Joy Harjo, *Poet Warrior: A Memoir* (Norton, 2021).

The Polish poet and Nobel laureate: Wisława Szymborska, "Utopia," in *Map: Collected and Last Poems*, trans. Clare Cavanagh and Stanisław Barańczak (Houghton Mifflin Harcourt, 2015).

The Certainty Trap

Those expectations begin: David Foster Wallace, "This Is Water," commencement speech, Kenyon College, Ohio, May 21, 2005, fs.blog/david-foster-wallace-this-is-water/.

Fear is described as: R. Nicholas Carleton, "Into the Unknown: A Review and Synthesis of Contemporary Models Involving Uncertainty," *Journal of Anxiety Disorders* 39 (April 2016): 30–43, doi.org/10.1016/j.janxdis.2016.02.007.

Feel the Fear

In her book *A Field Guide*: Rebecca Solnit, *A Field Guide to Getting Lost* (Penguin, 2005).

As H. P. Lovecraft wrote: H. P. Lovecraft, "Supernatural Horror in Literature," 1927, hplovecraft.com/writings/texts/essays/shil.aspx.

"The best way to combat fear": Justin Richmond (host), *Broken Record*, podcast, "Bonus: David Blaine with Rick Rubin," Pushkin, April 9, 2020, omny.fm/shows/broken-record-with-rick-rubin-malcolm-gladwell-bru/bonus-david-blaine-with-rick-rubin. All quotes from Blaine are taken from this podcast.

In an essay in *Scientific American*: Scott Barry Kaufman, "Who Created Maslow's Iconic Pyramid?" *Scientific American*, April 23, 2019, scientificamerican.com/blog/beautiful-minds/who-created-maslows-iconic-pyramid/.

As Maslow himself wrote: Abraham Maslow, *Motivation and Personality* (Harper & Row, 1954).

In her book *Feel the Fear*: Susan Jeffers, *Feel the Fear … and Do It Anyway: Dynamic Techniques for Turning Fear, Indecision, and Anger into Power, Action, and Love* (Harcourt, 1987).

In his *Letters from a Stoic*: Seneca, "On Groundless Fears," letter 13 in *Moral Letters to Lucilius* [also known as *Letters from a Stoic*], en.wikisource.org/wiki/Moral_letters_to_Lucilius/Letter_13.

As Yann Martel writes: Yann Martel, *Life of Pi* (Vintage Canada, 2002), 31.

What Are We Paying Attention To?

He decided, he told the *New Yorker*: David Remnick, "The Defiance of Salman Rushdie," *New Yorker*, February 6, 2023, newyorker.com/magazine/2023/02/13/salman-rushdie-recovery-victory-city.

If, as Susan Sontag wrote: Susan Sontag, *Illness as Metaphor* (Farrar, Straus & Giroux, 1978).

Attention, as Amishi P. Jha writes: Amishi P. Jha, *Peak Mind: Find Your Focus, Own Your Attention, Invest 12 Minutes a Day* (HarperOne, 2021).

Researchers in France: E. Veerapa, P. Grandgenevre, M. El Fayoumi, et al., "Attentional Bias Towards Negative Stimuli in Healthy Individuals and the Effects of Trait Anxiety," *Scientific Reports* 10, no. 11826 (2020), doi.org/10.1038/s41598-020-68490-5.

Harvard cognitive scientist: Steven Pinker, *Enlightenment Now: The Case for Reason, Science, Humanism, and Progress* (Penguin, 2018).

In his blog *Experimental History*: Adam M. Mastroianni and Daniel T. Gilbert, "The Illusion of Moral Decline," *Nature* 618 (2023): 782–89, nature.com/articles/s41586-023-06137-x.

"For most of us": Rachel Carson, "Help Your Child to Wonder," *Woman's Home Companion*, July 1956, rachelcarsoncouncil.org/wp-content/uploads/2019/08/whc_rc_sow_web.pdf.

Fred Rogers, an icon of comfort: "Remembering Mr. Rogers (1994/1997)," posted February 27, 2016, by Charlie Rose (YouTube channel), youtube.com/watch?v=djoyd46TVVc.

Research cited in *Psychological Science*: M. Rudd, K. D. Vohs, and J. Aaker, "Awe Expands People's Perception of Time, Alters Decision Making, and Enhances Well-Being," *Psychological Science* 23, no. 10 (2012): 1130–36, https://doi.org/10.1177/0956797612438731.

In his book *Awe*: Dacher Keltner, *Awe: The Transformative Power of Everyday Wonder* (Penguin, 2023).

British author G. K. Chesterton once wrote: G. K. Chesterton, *The Flying Stars and Other Stories* (n.p., 2013).

Your brain gets better: Norman Doidge, *The Brain That Changes Itself: Stories of Personal Triumph from the Frontiers of Brain Science* (Penguin, 2007).

"The art of being wise": William James, *The Principles of Psychology*, vol. 2 (Holt, 1890).

Speaking at a commencement address: Corinne Militello, "Commencement 2003," *Vassar: The Alumnae/i Quarterly*

99, no. 3 (Fall 2003), vassar.edu/vq/issues/2003/04/features/commencement.html.

"One thing I feel, well, proud of": Hadley Freeman, "Salman Rushdie: 'I Am Stupidly Optimistic—It Got Me Through Those Bad Years,'" *The Guardian*, May 15, 2021, theguardian.com/books/2021/may/15/salman-rushdie-i-am-stupidly-optimistic-it-got-me-through-those-bad-years.

Eighteen months after: Penguin Books, "'This was a necessary book for me to write …,'" Facebook, October 11, 2023, facebook.com/share/p/1C6u9WivGA/.

Getting Lost

"In every work of art": Ann Hamilton, "Making Not Knowing," in Mary Jane Jacob and Jacquelynn Baas, eds., *Learning Mind: Experience into Art* (University of California Press, 2010), sites.evergreen.edu/making2015/wp-content/uploads/sites/42/2014/12/Hamilton-Making-Not-Knowing.pdf. All quotes from Hamilton are taken from this essay.

"That is," he wrote: Hyder Edward Rollins, ed., *The Letters of John Keats, 1814–1821*, vol. 2 (Harvard University Press, 1958).

Herbie Hancock tells a story: "Playing Wrong Notes in Jazz—Herbie Hancock on Miles Davis, a Fantastic Story About Mistakes," posted October 7, 2020, by Mike del Ferro—Music (YouTube channel), youtu.be/m6fVZtp9vGQ. All quotes from Hancock are taken from this video.

"Curiously," he writes: Rick Rubin, *The Creative Act: A Way of Being* (Penguin, 2023), 120.

"You cannot be playful": John Cleese, "Creativity in Management," lecture delivered to Video Arts, 1991, juliesaffrin.com/wp-content/uploads/2013/08/John-Cleese.pdf.

States of Panic

The painful uncertainty and struggle: Mary Oliver, "The Summer Day," in *New and Selected Poems*, vol. 1 (Beacon, 1992), 94.

"People develop new understandings": Lorna Collier, "Growth After Trauma: Why Are Some People More Resilient than Others—and Can It Be Taught?" *Monitor on Psychology* 47, no. 10 (November 2016), apa.org/monitor/2016/11/growth-trauma.

"By blurring the line": James Vincent, "US Lawmakers Say AI Deepfakes 'Have the Potential to Disrupt Every Facet of Our Society,'" *The Verge*, September 14, 2018, theverge.com/2018/9/14/17859188/ai-deepfakes-national-security-threat-lawmakers-letter-intelligence-community.

Add to the equation: Thomas Claburn, "The Launch of ChatGPT Polluted the World Forever, Like the First Atomic Weapons Tests," *The Register*, June 15, 2025, theregister.com/2025/06/15/ai_model_collapse_pollution/.

At a 2017 conference: Future of Life Institute, "Asilomar AI Principles," August 11, 2017, futureoflife.org/open-letter/ai-principles/.

"Despite the growing role": Robert K. Heinssen, Carol R. Glass, and Luanne A. Knight, "Assessing Computer Anxiety:

Development and Validation of the Computer Anxiety Rating Scale," *Computers in Human Behavior* 3, no. 1 (1987), doi.org/10.1016/0747-5632(87)90010-0.

And the human technicians: Chris Hannay, "How AI Went from Dooming Radiologists to Making Them Better," *Globe and Mail*, December 10, 2024, theglobeandmail.com/business/article-how-ai-went-from-dooming-radiologists-to-making-them-better/.

"We were able to take": Mark Savage, "Sir Paul McCartney Says Artificial Intelligence Has Enabled a 'Final' Beatles Song," BBC, June 13, 2023, bbc.com/news/entertainment-arts-65881813.

For Rick Rubin: Rubin, *Creative Act*, 120.

As Hellen Keller wrote: Helen Keller, *Optimism: An Essay* (T. Y. Crowell, 1903).

A Climate of Crisis

Most upsetting is the number of children: Britt Wray, excerpt from a speech to the fourteenth World Economic Forum's Annual Meeting of the New Champions, Tianjin, China, June 2023, Unthinkable Times, July 3, 2023, unthinkable.substack.com/p/read-britts-speech-to-the-world-economic.

It's a widespread condition: "New APA Poll Reveals That Americans Are Increasingly Anxious About Climate Change's Impact on Planet, Mental Health," press release, American Psychiatric Association, October 21, 2020, psychiatry.org/news-room/news-releases/climate-poll-2020.

"Recognizing that emotions": Ashlee Cunsolo et al., "Ecological Grief and Anxiety: The Start of a Healthy Response to Climate Change?" *Lancet* 4, no. 7 (July 2020), thelancet.com/journals/lanplh/article/PIIS2542-5196(20)30144-3/fulltext.

Britt Wray argues: Anna Sale (host), *Death, Sex & Money*, podcast, episode 345, "How Much Climate Anxiety Helps?" Slate, May 11, 2022, slate.com/podcasts/death-sex-money/2022/05/how-much-climate-anxiety-helps.

As they wrote of their findings: Huanhuan Zhao et al., "Relation Between Awe and Environmentalism: The Role of Social Dominance Orientation," *Frontiers in Psychology* 9, no. 2367 (December 3, 2018), doi.org/10.3389/fpsyg.2018.02367.

"People need to feel the discomfort": Cassandra Drudi, "In *Generation Dread*, Britt Wray Encourages Those Experiencing Eco-Anxiety to Turn Their Feelings into Action," *Quill & Quire*, June 15, 2022, quillandquire.com/authors/in-generation-dread-britt-wray-encourages-those-experiencing-eco-anxiety-to-turn-their-feelings-into-action/.

Flying by the Seat of Our Pants

"The more you learn about poker": "Why Being Uncertain Is a Hidden Strength," video, *Big Think*, 2023, bigthink.com/the-well/the-power-of-saying-i-dont-know/.

As Ursula K. Le Guin beautifully put it: Ursula K. Le Guin, *The Wave in the Mind: Talks and Essays on the Writer, the Reader, and the Imagination* (Shambhala, 2004).

Pro Tempore

"I'd thought I was in limbo": Amanda Knox (@amandaknox), Twitter (now X) post, February 24, 2023, x.com/amandaknox/status/1629181705830670336. All quotes from Knox are taken from this thread.

Austrian psychiatrist and Holocaust survivor: Viktor E. Frankl, *Man's Search for Meaning* (1946; Beacon, 2006) and *Yes to Life: In Spite of Everything* (1946; Beacon, 2020).

"Sometimes you're doing really well": Simon Hattenstone, "Patti Smith: Punk Poet Queen," *The Guardian*, May 25, 2013, theguardian.com/music/2013/may/25/patti-smith-interview-punk-poet.

"Illness frightens us": Emily St. John Mandel, *Sea of Tranquility* (HarperCollins, 2022), 83.

Illness is, as Susan Sontag called it: Susan Sontag, *Illness as Metaphor* (Vintage, 1979), 3.

German philosopher Friedrich Nietzsche: Friedrich Nietzsche, *Ecco Homo: How What Becomes What One Is* (n.p., 1908).

"Mister Duffy lived": James Joyce, *Dubliners* (Grant Richards, 1914).

To treat life: Somerset Maugham, *A Writer's Notebook* (Knopf, 2012), 84.

The American physician: Oliver Wendell Holmes Sr., "The Chambered Nautilus," 1858, poetryfoundation.org/poems/44379/the-chambered-nautilus.

Answers and Questions

In her 2007 "chambermaid study": A. J. Crum and E. Langer, "Mind-Set Matters: Exercise and the Placebo Effect," *Psychological Science* 18, no. 2 (2007): 165–71, doi.org/10.1111/j.1467-9280.2007.01867.x.

In a research paper: Tanisha G. Hill-Jarrett, "The Black Radical Imagination: A Space of Hope and Possible Futures," *Frontiers in Neurology* 14 (2023), doi.org/10.3389/fneur.2023.1241922.

In his award-winning book: Chris Turner, *How to Be a Climate Optimist: Blueprints for a Better World* (Random House Canada, 2022).

Suffering, Chödrön writes: Pema Chödrön, *When Things Fall Apart: Heart Advice for Difficult Times* (Shambhala, 2002).

"You must never confuse faith": Boris Groysberg and Robin Abrahams, "What the Stockdale Paradox Tells Us About Crisis Leadership," *Working Knowledge*, Harvard Business School newsletter, August 17, 2020, library.hbs.edu/working-knowledge/what-the-stockdale-paradox-tells-us-about-crisis-leadership.

"Our life experience will equal": James, *Principles of Psychology*, vol. 2.

GILLIAN DEACON is an award-winning broadcaster and writer. A familiar voice on CBC Radio, Gill spent over a decade as host of *Here & Now*, Toronto's afternoon drive show on CBC Radio One. She is the author of the national bestsellers *There's Lead in Your Lipstick: Toxins in Everyday Bodycare and How to Avoid Them*; *Green for Life*; and the memoir *Naked Imperfection*. Gill lives in Toronto with her husband and their three sons.

@gilldeacon
aloveaffairwiththeunknown.substack.com
gilldeacon.ca
A Love Affair with the Unknown is an Apple featured podcast. Subscribe wherever you get your podcasts.